SWIFT AS A SHADOW

TEXT BY THE STAFF OF NATURALIS, NATIONAAL NATUURHISTORISCH MUSEUM, LEIDEN

Lars van den Hoek Ostende, *Educational Officer*

Dr. Chris Smeenk, *Curator of Mammals*

Dr. René Dekker, *Curator of Birds*

Dr. Marinus Hoogmoed, *Curator of Reptiles and Amphibians*

Dr. Martien van Oijen, *Curator of Fishes*

PHOTOGRAPHS BY

ROSAMOND PURCELL

SWIFT AS A SHADOW

EXTINCT AND ENDANGERED ANIMALS

AFTERWORD BY ROSS D.E. MacPHEE, PH.D.

Chairman and Curator, Department of Mammalogy,

American Museum of Natural History

DESIGN BY CHRISTOPHER MOISAN

A Mariner Original

Houghton Mifflin Company

Boston | New York

1999

With the following exceptions, all of the photographs were taken in the collection of
Naturalis, Nationaal Natuurhistorisch Museum, Leiden:

Museum of Comparative Zoology, Harvard University:

Bald eagle • Solenodon • Gibbon • Squirrel monkey • Moa (piled bones) • Javan tiger (paws on pelt)

Bishop Museum, Honolulu, Hawaii:

Green sea turtle • Hawaiian land snails • Birdwing butterflies

Texts edited by Kara Moritz and Chris Smeenk

Rosamond Purcell would like to give special thanks to Hanna Shell, Lisa Melandri,
and Jenna Terry.

Art direction by Steven Cooley

Production by Terry McAweeney

Purcell, Rosamond Wolff.

Swift as a shadow : extinct and endangered animals / photographs
by Rosamond Purcell.

p. cm.

Includes bibliographical references (p.) and index.

ISBN 0-395-89228-7

1. Extinct animals. 2. Endangered species. 3. Extinct animals—Pictorial works.

4. Endangered animals—Pictorial works. I. Title.

QL88.P87 1999

591.68—dc21 99-18095 CIP

PRINTED IN HONG KONG

DNP 10 9 8 7 6 5 4 3 2 1

CONTENTS :

" Swift as a shadow . . .

The extinct and endangered animals shown on these pages are mostly to be found in the world-renowned collections
of the Nationaal Natuurhistorisch Museum (National Museum of Natural History) in Leiden, the Netherlands;
the others are in Bishop Museum, Honolulu, Hawaii, or the Museum of Comparative Zoology, Harvard University,
Cambridge, Massachusetts. They are presented here in two groups, according to their historical or current habitats:
continental animals and island and marine animals.

. . . short as any dream"
— William Shakespeare, A MIDSUMMER NIGHT'S DREAM

CONTINENTAL ANIMALS :

{ *Conuropsis carolinensis* }

CAROLINA PARAKEET EXTINCT

Incas, the last Carolina parakeet, died in his cage in the Cincinnati Zoo on February 21, 1918, only six months after the death of Lady Jane, his companion of thirty-two years. At the beginning of the nineteenth century, the Carolina parakeet, with its yellow neck and blazing orange crown, ranged from Mexico to New York State. It was the only parrot to adapt successfully to the harsh winters of eastern North America, yet the rapid destruction of America's woodlands for farmland destroyed its favorite habitat. Tempted from the forests, flocks of up to three hundred parrots would swiftly descend and consume fruit farms' entire harvests. The birds were shot to protect crops, for sport, and for their colorful feathers, which were popular on ladies' hats. These social little parakeets would fly squawking around a wounded or dead companion rather than deserting it, which enabled hunters to pick them off one by one.

{ *Ectopistes migratorius* }

PASSENGER PIGEON
EXTINCT

With feathers that flickered green or purple according to the light, the passenger pigeon had a long, slender tail, pointed wings, and a graceful, powerful body. In the 1830s, the American ornithologist John James Audubon wrote that as flocks of the birds passed swiftly overhead, "the light of noonday was obscured as by an eclipse" and the noise reminded him of "a hard gale at sea passing through the rigging of a close-reefed vessel." Trees were uprooted under the sheer weight of landing pigeons, and breeding colonies blanketed treetops over as much as forty miles. Yet in the span of a human lifetime the passenger pigeon was gone. During the nineteenth century, hundreds of thousands of birds were sold to the meat markets of New York City. Hunting for sport was devastating to the species; in one competition the winner had to kill more than 30,000 birds to claim his prize. By the 1890s the pigeons were scarce. As flocks dwindled, chicks became easier prey for predators and birds could not produce enough offspring to replace themselves. On September 1, 1914, Martha, the last passenger pigeon, died in the Cincinnati Zoo.

{ *Gymnogyps californicus* }

CALIFORNIA CONDOR

The California condor, with a wingspan approaching ten feet, is the largest flying bird in North America. In prehistoric times these birds ranged over most of coastal North America, scavenging the carcasses of woolly mammoths and giant sloths.

The cultivation of California led to the species' rapid decline. Poisoned carcasses set out by ranchers to kill coyotes and squirrels, lead poisoning from the shot in carrion, collisions with power lines, hunting, and residential development all brought this ancient vulture to the verge of extinction. In a desperate attempt to save the condor through a captive breeding program, biologists captured the total wild population, consisting of only nine birds, between 1985 and 1987. Since then the population has grown. In 1992 the effort to return the birds to the wild began, but most died shortly after their release. By 1997, the number of live condors had risen to 133, of which 33 live in the wild.

{ Ophrysia superciliosa }

PRESUMED EXTINCT

HIMALAYAN MOUNTAIN QUAIL

The first description of the Himalayan mountain quail, based on a bird
kept in a private Liverpool aviary, was published in 1846. The origins
of this bird are mysterious, but the species is thought to have lived in
the grass and scrub along the steep foothills of the western Himalayas,
at altitudes between five and six thousand feet. Although the last
reliable report of the bird appeared in 1876, there have been regular
unconfirmed sightings, most recently in 1993. It is possible that this
elusive quail still survives, hidden in the vast ranges of the Himalayas.

04

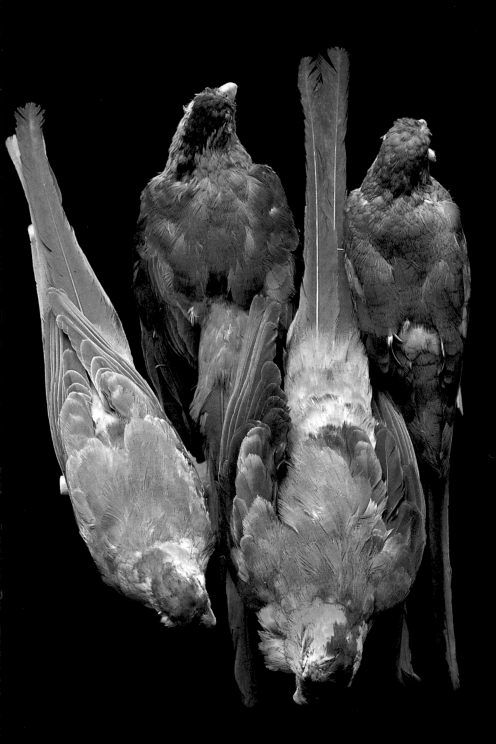

PARADISE PARROT

In 1884 the British ornithologist William
Thomas Greene wrote in his book *Parrots
in Captivity*: "No one can see the Paradise
Parrot without desiring to possess so beautiful and graceful a bird . . . but alas! one in
a dozen survives a few months and — dies
suddenly in a fit." Already threatened with
capture and exportation as a caged bird,
this elegant Australian parrot was dealt
a fatal blow by the introduction of cattle,
which depleted the supply of grass seed
available for food. C. C. Jerrard, who pho-
tographed one of the last wild pairs in the
1920s, described the male parrot's song:
"His whole body vibrated with the force
and intensity of his musical effort, imparting
an agitated motion to the long tail which
bore adequate testimony to the vim of the
performance. It all seemed to indicate a
very intense little personality under the
beautiful exterior."

{ *Psephotus pulcherrimus* }

EXTINCT
SPIX'S MACAW

The history of the Leiden specimens of
Spix's macaw reflects the major threat
to the species: all the skins are from birds
that died in captivity. Rare since its discovery by Europeans, the Spix's macaw
was threatened by the colonization of
inland Brazil, which destroyed its wood-
land habitat for farmland. The growth of
the pet trade brought another danger.
Small populations were living in Brazil as
recently as the 1970s, but demand for
these exquisite macaws kept prices high
and trappers active. By 1998, the species

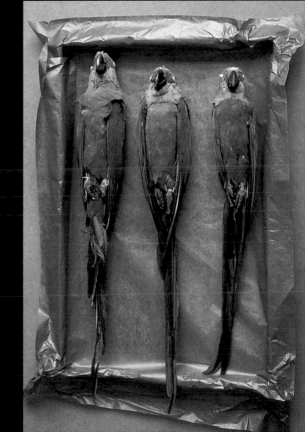

{ Rhodonessa caryophyllacea }

The pink-headed duck lived in the formerly impenetrable swamps of the Ganges and Brahmaputra rivers in northern India. It was always considered rare, but this may be due to the remoteness of its watery haunts. As the swamps became cultivated, the duck was at first seen more often. Soon, however, swamp reclamation forced it into the range of hunters' rifles. Its bright pink head made it a valuable trophy, and although British colonialists disliked the flavor of its meat, the fast-growing local population may not have been so particular. Around the end of the nineteenth century it was often seen for sale in the markets of Calcutta. The last pink-headed duck probably died in the 1940s, in a British aviary far from its native swamps.

PINK-HEADED DUCK EXTINCT

06

GLAUCOUS MACAW EXTINCT

{ *Anodorhynchus glaucus* }

In 1989 the Brazilian ornithologist Antonio Silva claimed he knew a secret site where a small population of glaucous macaws still survived. Despite this claim, the glaucous macaw is generally considered extinct. The species once lived in the border area of Brazil, Argentina, and Paraguay and probably also in northwestern Uruguay. Naturalists exploring the interior by boat spotted it along riverbanks, but it may have also inhabited wooded savannas. Some scientists believe that natural factors caused its decline, while others blame land reclamation over the past century. The last reliable sighting was in 1955. Searches by ornithologists in Paraguay in the late 1970s found no trace of the bird, nor have there been any reports by traders, who are well aware of the enormous amount of money they could receive for a live glaucous macaw.

07

Living high in the forest canopy, the kinglet calyptura of Brazil forages in pairs for insects and berries. Its call, described as "short, raw, and unpleasant," is remarkably loud for such a tiny creature. The bird was not seen for nearly a century, probably because of its small size and secluded habitat, but was rediscovered in 1996. Its range is restricted to an area close to Rio de Janeiro, and this habitat is threatened by the rapid growth of the city and suburbs, which has already destroyed some of the forest in which it lives.

{ *Hippotragus leucophaeus* }

EXTINCT

BLAAUWBOK, OR BLUE ANTELOPE

Long ago in the lush green south of Africa, a small, blue-hued
antelope grazed over the grassy countryside. The range of the
blaauwbok, or blue antelope, was already limited when the
animal was first seen by seventeenth- and eighteenth-century
European settlers in the Cape Colony. The change of grassland
into bush and forest as the climate became warmer and the
introduction of livestock may have contributed to a decline in
the population two thousand years ago. Dutch cultivation and
firearm hunting in the Cape Colony insured that the last herds
of blaauwbok were gone by 1800. Few natural history collectors
had a chance to obtain specimens of this graceful antelope,
the first African mammal to become extinct in modern times.
The Leiden specimen is one of the oldest preserved mounted
animal skins in the world, and is the only surviving skin used
for the formal description of the species in 1766.

09

{ *Canis lupus nubilis* }

Only a few centuries ago, wolves were found throughout the Northern Hemisphere. In the United States, as settlers moved westward, they launched intensive eradication campaigns against the wolf. A government-supported system of bounties, poisonings, and other population control programs wiped out the animal in over 95 percent of the areas where it had once roamed. One subspecies, the Great Plains wolf, which ranged from Missouri to the Dakotas and up into southern Canada, is now extinct. This large wolf followed the endless herds of prairie bison, preying on the young and the sickly. With the coming of the railways, the bison suffered a massive onslaught. As the wolves' food supply dwindled, they were forced to prey on cattle. This proved fatal, since the wolves were subsequently killed by farmers protecting their livestock, by trappers for their pelts, and by settlers simply from fear. The exact date of extinction of the Great Plains wolf is unknown.

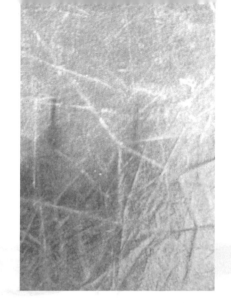

GREAT PLAINS WOLF EXTINCT

10

{ Equus burchellii burchellii }

Pale brown "shadow stripes" appeared within the white stripes of Burchell's zebra, or dauw, the southernmost of the "plains zebras." Like other zebras in this group, dauws populated the African plains in great numbers, and settlers reported seeing groups of thousands. The dauw population was destroyed by factors that also wiped out its relative the quagga: overhunting, the cultivation of land, and competition with farm animals for grazing land, particularly in periods of drought. The last captive animal died in the London Zoo in 1910, several years after this lovely zebra had disappeared from the wild.

EXTINCT
BURCHELL'S ZEBRA, OR DAUW

11

EXTINCT **QUAGGA**

{ *Equus quagga* }

There is now evidence that the quagga was a form of Burchell's zebra, though it was originally classified as a species in its own right. Its dark stripes fused together toward the hind part of its body, and its legs, tail, and abdomen were plain white or pale cream. At one time great numbers of this unusual zebra grazed over the South African plains. The quaggas' flashy skins were used for various purposes, and their meat served as food for Hottentot servants. Overgrazing of the plains by livestock depleted the zebras' food supply. Quaggas were easy to keep in captivity; on South African farms an in London they were used for drawing carts. Yet the last quagga, a mare, died in 1883 in the Amsterdam Zoo, before a successful breeding program was established.

12

EXTINCT
BARBARY LION

{ *Panthera leo leo* }

Lions once ranged throughout Europe and the Middle East, as evidenced by many references to the great cats in the Bible and in Greek mythology. As their domain contracted, populations of subspecies such as the Barbary lion became extinct. This lion roamed North Africa from Tripoli through Tunisia and Algeria to Morocco. Its mane, which covered nearly half its body, was brown, except for a yellow fringe around the face. The Romans may have used the Barbary lion in their brutal coliseum shows. Although hunting played a role in the lion's extinction, ecological change caused by farming is thought to have been the major cause. Well-guarded herds of cattle destroyed forests, and food supplies of deer and gazelle disappeared. In Algeria, the Turks encouraged the killing of lions by paying well for their skins. During the French occupation, the price went down to only 50 francs a skin, yet many Frenchmen became relentless hunters, killing more than two hundred lions in Algeria between 1873 and 1883. The last Barbary lions were shot between 1920 and 1930 in their final stronghold, the rugged Atlas Mountains of Morocco.

13

EXTINCT
CAPE LION

{ *Panthera leo melanochaitus* }

Lions disappeared from Europe around A.D. 100. In Asia, only a few lions remain, confined to the Gir Forest sanctuary in India. The range of lions in Africa has also diminished. None survive in North Africa, and in South Africa original populations live only in the Kruger and Kalahari Gemsbok national parks. The South African Cape lion, recognizable in the works of Rembrandt, is extinct. The largest and darkest of all lions, males had a heavy mane stretching over the abdomen, nearly black but for a brown fringe around the face. Once common around Cape Town, this lion lived in the former Cape Province and the southern Orange Free State of South Africa. Advancing European colonists wiped out the vast herds of game that served as the Cape lion's main food source, and although the exact date of extinction is unknown, this majestic lion had probably disappeared by 1860.

Very little is known about the white-footed rabbit-rat, a nocturnal rodent that lived in the eucalypt woodlands and open forests of southeastern Australia and the Port Phillip region of Victoria. The cause of its extinction around 1875 is presumed to be the European settlers' introduction of predators such as cats and foxes. The British zoologist John Gould wrote of collecting white-footed rabbit-rats by simply cutting off branches of the hollow trees where they slept in nests of dry leaves during the day. A governor of South Australia, Sir George Grey, once sent a specimen to Gould. In an accompanying letter, Grey described behavior more typical of marsupials than of rodents: "The specimen I send to you, a female, had three young ones attached to its teats when it was caught . . . On pulling the young from the teats of the dead mother, they seized hold of my glove with the mouth and held on so strongly that it was difficult to disengage them."

{ *Conilurus albipes* }

EXTINCT **WHITE-FOOTED RABBIT-RAT**

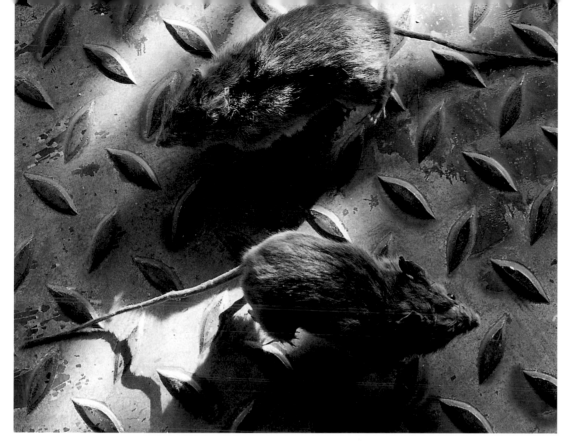

14

GOULD'S MOUSE EXTINCT

{ Pseudomys gouldii }

Gould's mouse once made elaborate burrows in the sandhills and loosely packed soil of the Australian plains. Up to eight animals would live together in these warrens, sometimes sharing the same nest of dry grass. Judging from finds in owl pellets, at one time this mouse was widespread. Presumably the decline of Gould's mouse took place in the first part of the nineteenth century, although the cause is unclear. The Blandowski Expedition of 1856 collected the last known Gould's mouse at the junction of the Murray and Darling rivers in southeastern Australia.

The pig-footed bandicoot was named for its forefoot, which had only two functional toes. A small, slender-legged marsupial that fed on plants and insects, it once roamed the semi-arid regions of southern and central Australia. The species appears to have been in decline before European settlers arrived in the nineteenth century, and the causes of its extinction remain unknown. The last known pig-footed bandicoot was captured in 1907, but the species may have survived into the 1950s.

{ *Chaeropus ecaudatus* }

PIG-FOOTED BANDICOOT EXTINCT

LONG-TAILED HOPPING-MOUSE EXTINCT

{ Notomys longicaudatus }

15

Little is known about the long-tailed hopping-mouse, which was once common in much of southern and central Australia. The animals lived in mounds of earth dug up by bilbies and burrowing bettongs, and it may be that the disappearance of the latter species contributed to the extinction of this mouse. Though a living long-tailed hopping-mouse has not been seen since 1901, some believe that the species may still survive in the wilderness of the central continent.

BANDED HARE-WALLABY   ENDANGERED
{ *Lagostrophus fasciatus* }
TASMANIAN BETTONG   ENDANGERED
{ *Bettongia gaimardi* }

The banded hare-wallaby was once abundant in southern Australia, but European settlement of the continent brought an immediate decline of the species. (Two specimens are shown in the center of this picture.) It is an especially aggressive species: males fight savagely to defend their territory and food. The banded hare-wallaby still survives on Shark Bay's Dorre and Bernier islands, although unconfirmed mainland sightings continued into the nineteenth century.

The three Tasmanian bettongs pictured here are similar in size to rabbits. The bettong was once the most prevalent mammal in many areas of Australia, but the population declined in the nineteenth century, probably because of the arrival of the fox. Rabbits, grazing cattle, and cultivation may also have played a role in the Tasmanian bettong's fate by destroying grasslands. Unlike other small marsupials, the species persisted on the mainland into the twentieth century. Today it survives only on a few fox-free islands off the west coast of Australia. In Tasmania the bettong lives in dry, open forests.

{ Thylacinus cynocephalus }

The thylacine, commonly known as the Tasmanian tiger, was the largest carnivorous marsupial to survive into historic times. With a skull remarkably like that of a wolf, the thylacine could open its jaws to an angle of 150 degrees — wider than many other mammals can. It carried its young in a pouch and preyed on other marsupials, such as kangaroos and wallabies. The species disappeared from mainland Australia and New Guinea sometime after the last ice age. It was common in remote parts of Tasmania until the early nineteenth century, when European settlers, fearing that it killed sheep, began to hunt it mercilessly. Records indicate that between 1888 and 1914, hunters shot a total of 2,268 thylacines. An epidemic may have been the final blow. The last captive thylacine died in Tasmania's Hobart Zoo in 1936. Over the years there have been many unconfirmed reports of sightings and tracks. A lair was discovered in 1966, though there was no way to tell when it had last been used.

THYLACINE EXTINCT

AMERICAN BALD EAGLE
THREATENED, FORMERLY ENDANGERED

{ *Haliaeetus leucocephalus* }

Once plentiful near lakes and coasts throughout North America, bald eagles began to decline in numbers during the nineteenth century. Trophy hunters prized the bird's classic white head and seven-foot wingspan. Habitat loss, the cutting of nesting trees, poisoning, and electrocution by high wires also threatened the eagle's survival. Although the United States government began protecting the bird in 1940, the pesticide DDT almost destroyed it by fatally weakening the linings of eggshells. DDT was banned in 1972, and since the 1980s the population has resurged, as a result of both the reintroduction of eagles to their traditional ranges and habitat protection. Illegal hunting remains the primary threat to the United States' national bird.

The colored plate of the bald eagle on the facing page, from the artist Alexander Wilson's 1812 book *American Ornithology*, shows the specimen in the Peale Collection at the Museum of Comparative Zoology at Harvard University.

18

White-headed Eagle

{ *Haplochromis* spp. }

CICHLID FISH OF LAKE VICTORIA EXTINCT

Scientists believe that approximately 14,000 years ago, Lake Victoria, which lies in a basin in central Africa, dried up. When the water returned to the lake, it was colonized by a few river fish of the genus *Haplochromis*. There followed a burst of evolution resulting in more than four hundred species of these cichlid fish, each with its own feeding habits. Because of this astonishingly rapid speciation, Lake Victoria has been called "Darwin's pond."

Haplochromis are between two and ten inches long. The males are brightly colored. The more inconspicuous females carry their eggs and young in their mouths, which makes them particularly vulnerable to overfishing. Unfortunately, many species from Lake Victoria that are only now being formally described are already extinct. The cause is the large, predatory Nile perch, a deep-water fish introduced in the early 1960s to increase the yield of the local fishery. A few years after a sudden, unexplained increase in the numbers of perch, almost all of the more than two hundred species of *Haplochromis* living in water deeper than twelve feet had vanished.

This little monkey, a native of the São João river basin in Brazil,
is covered in silky golden fur and looks like a miniature lion. Only
four hundred golden lion tamarins still exist in the wild, and they are
threatened by capture and domestication: their spectacular coats make
them desirable pets. They prefer to live in the middle layers of ancient
forests, where they shelter inside old tree trunks, behind entrances
too narrow to admit most predators. The destruction of the rain forest
has forced many of the remaining lion tamarins into areas of younger
growth, where there are fewer hollows for them to hide in. Sadly, it
is believed that the tamarins of today's new forests are smaller than
those found in ancient rain forests, and their fur is less shiny.

{ *Leontopithecus rosalia* }

GOLDEN LION TAMARIN
ENDANGERED
20

ENDANGERED **GIBBON**

{ *Hylobates concolor* }

The ancient Chinese believed the gibbon was a sylvan sprite, and the Dayaks of Borneo imbued these animals with magical powers. It is said that in 600 B.C., a king in the Yangtze River Valley had the entire forest near his capital cleared to search for his lost pet gibbon. These graceful primates, with their long arms and bare black faces, are thought to have diverged from the ancestral stock even earlier than apes and humans. They live in monogamous family groups, much as humans do. They swing arm over arm through the forest canopy with amazing speed and agility, and throughout the forests of Southeast Asia they are known for their vocal outbursts, which are a form of territorial display. Because they live on a diet of fresh fruit, which varies from season to season and is available in widely scattered areas, gibbons require a vast territory. Habitat loss and illegal hunting pose a threat to all eleven species.

{ Chiropotes satanas }

This bearded saki species provides a good example of what can happen when a preserved specimen no longer looks like the living creature. In 1848 taxonomists named this monkey the "white-nosed saki" on the basis of a skin that had dried and faded. When the animal is alive, it in fact has a bright red nose. The black bearded saki is dark and has a long, thick tail and short, soft fur. Both sexes have beards, and the males have bulbous swellings on the tops of their heads. These medium-sized monkeys live in the tall, virgin rain forest of the Amazon Basin in groups of ten to thirty, whistling to one another through the upper levels of the canopy. They use their strong, protruding teeth like beaks to break open the husks of Brazil nuts and hard fruits. Bearded sakis are hunted for their meat, which is considered a delicacy, and reportedly their tails are used as dusters.

ENDANGERED BLACK BEARDED SAKI

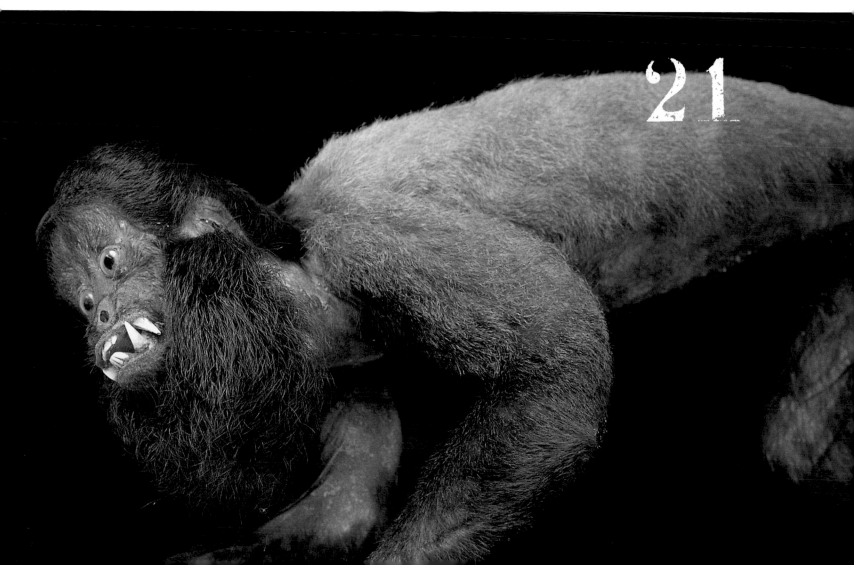

'21

22

{ *Saguinus oedipus* }   { *Gorilla gorilla* }

COTTON-TOPPED TAMARIN AND GORILLA
ENDANGERED   ENDANGERED

Found only in northwestern Colombia, cotton-topped tamarins are New World primates distinguishable by their white crown, red rump, and black tail. They are also called Liszt monkeys, because of their flowing white crest, which they raise and lower to threaten other animals. Cotton-topped tamarins live in highly cooperative groups of three to thirteen, feeding on fruit, insects, and spiders. After females give birth, usually to twins, males and other females become the primary caregivers, carrying the infants on their backs and returning them to their mothers only to nurse. These monkeys are often used as laboratory animals, and they are popular pets because of their endearing faces and exotic plumes.

The cotton-topped tamarin in this photograph — about the size of a squirrel — is shown with the hand of the largest primate, a gorilla. Despite the writings of such researchers as Dale Peterson, George Schaller, and Dian Fossey, which brought the plight of gorillas to public attention many years ago, all gorilla populations are seriously endangered today.

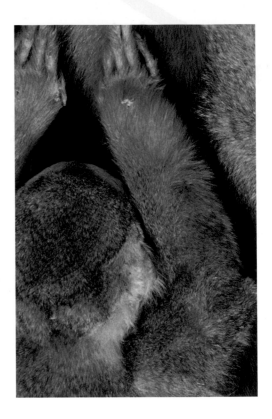

SQUIRREL MONKEY

Squirrel monkeys can be heard chattering to each other in the middle canopy of rain forests throughout the American tropics. There are several species of these monkeys, well known around the world as pets and laboratory animals. *Saimiri oerstedii*, a Central American species, is endangered. All species have elegant white faces accentuated by a peak of dark fur on the forehead and a dark patch on the muzzle. They are expert at balancing on palm fronds and collecting fruit from the ends of branches. In what may be the largest gatherings of nonhuman primates on earth, communities of two to five hundred individuals have been reported in untouched areas of the rain forest. Adult females form the core of the group. A childless female will often bond with a new mother and infant, becoming a sort of aunt to the newborn.

{ *Saimiri oerstedii* }

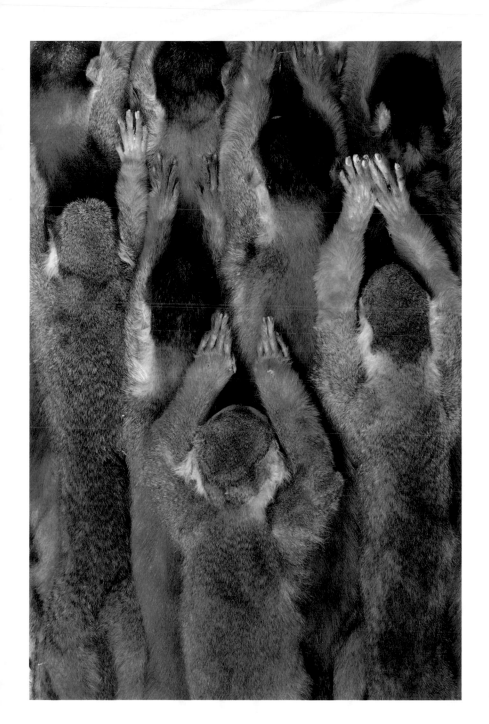

23

24

RHINOCEROS

ENDANGERED

{ *Rhinoceros* spp. }

There are five species of rhinoceros: African white, Indian, African black, Javan, and Sumatran. Many legends surround this "living fossil." Chewing rhinoceros meat is said to cure dysentery; the Nepalese drink the animal's urine to cure asthma and epilepsy; the umbilical stump is boiled to make a soup that heals rheumatism and arthritis; and rhinoceros horn is valued throughout Asia as an aphrodisiac, a poison detector, and a remedy for stomach ailments and flu. Fed by such beliefs, market demand and high prices for horns frustrate the animals' protectors. Hunters capture rhinos to cut off their horns, and such illegal poaching has reduced the wild population to barely two thousand animals. A solitary creature that requires a vast undisturbed territory, the rhino is also threatened by continuing habitat fragmentation, and many populations are on the verge of extinction.

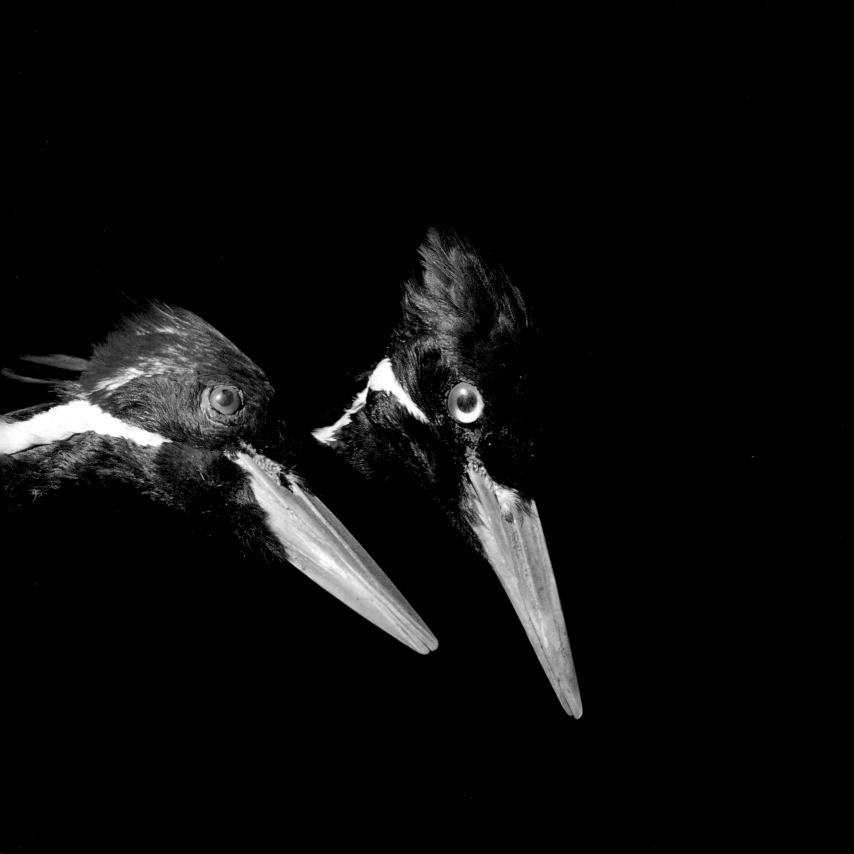

{ *Campephilus principalis* }

EXTINCT

25

IVORY-BILLED WOODPECKER

The elusive ivory-billed woodpecker was at home in the dark forests of the southern United States. With its brilliant blue-black feathers, white-patched wings, and bright red crest, it was one of the largest and most powerful of all woodpeckers. Its three-inch, ivory-colored bill could pierce bark up to eight inches deep with a single blow. Yet ivory-billed woodpeckers were very vulnerable. A single pair needed six square miles of wet forest with large dead trees in which to nest and search for grubs and beetles. The last known population in the United States disappeared in 1948, when a Louisiana forest was cleared to make room for a soy plantation. The Cuban subspecies survived longer, but by 1970 land cultivation had reduced this population to eight pairs at most. Explorers in the mountains near Moa in the early 1990s discovered fresh signs of feeding and caught a glimpse of a bird that may have been the ivory-bill. Since then, surveys have found no trace of this majestic woodpecker.

This small sea duck's nest and eggs have never been identified with certainty, although most likely its breeding area was on the Labrador peninsula. No one is quite sure why the Labrador duck disappeared. It wintered along the coasts of New England, New Jersey, and Long Island, and like other waterfowl, it was occasionally hunted and sold in the meat markets of New York and Baltimore, despite its unpleasant taste. Its peculiar beak suggests that it had specialized feeding habits and probably lived on small snails. Increasing human impact on the coasts of eastern North America may have caused a decline in several species of shellfish, eventually robbing the Labrador duck of its food supply. The last recorded sighting of the species was of a male caught off Long Island in 1875.

{ *Camptorhynchus labradorius* }

LABRADOR DUCK
EXTINCT

ISLAND AND MARINE ANIMALS :

{ Aepyornis maximus }

In 1658, Étienne de Flacourt, the first French governor of Madagascar, wrote of a giant bird that lived deep in the remotest reaches of the island. Recent excavations have shown that there were once several species of elephant bird in Madagascar. As in the case of the New Zealand moas, scientists believe that climatological changes combined with the impact of human settlement gradually wiped out these hulking, ostrichlike birds. Only the largest elephant bird, *Aepyornis maximus*, possibly survived in isolated valleys when the French claimed the island in 1642. Over ten feet tall, it was shorter than the tallest New Zealand moas, but bulkier, weighing up to a thousand pounds. It laid the biggest egg on record, over a foot long and equal in volume to 7 ostrich eggs (one of which is pictured here), 180 chicken eggs, or more than 12,000 hummingbird eggs. This monstrous bird and egg may have inspired the Arabian legend of the rukh, whose immense egg Sinbad encountered in *The Thousand and One Nights.*

ELEPHANT BIRD EXTINCT

GREAT AUK EXTINCT

{ Pinguinus impennis }

As recently as five hundred years ago, enormous colonies of great auks nested on rocky islands in the North Atlantic. These large flightless birds, called the "penguins of the North," had long black beaks and small wings. Though agile in water, they were slow and defenseless on land. Eaten by fisherman and whalers, auks were later also hunted for their feathers, which were used in feather beds. To loosen their plumage, the birds were boiled in large caldrons over fires fed with the oil of auks killed before them.

In 1830 a volcano erupted off the southwestern tip of Iceland, submerging the increasingly rare auk's last stronghold, the island of Geirfuglasker. European museums and collectors clamored for stuffed specimens and eggs of the nearly extinct bird, offering high prices to hunters. The last great auk hunt was in 1844 on the island of Eldey, off southwestern Iceland, when a pair was beaten to death and their egg was destroyed.

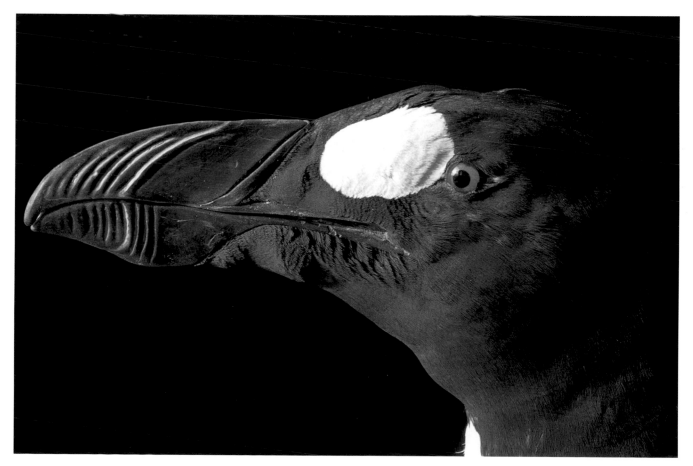

CUBAN RED MACAW

EXTINCT

{ *Ara tricolor* }

Young Cuban red macaws were often taken from the wild to be caged birds. Local people also ate this striking red parrot, and both factors led to its extinction. It lived in Cuba and Hispaniola, and some believe that it also inhabited Jamaica. Little is known of its habits; it probably fed on nuts, seeds, fruits, and shoots, as most macaws do. The last record of the Cuban red macaw was of a bird shot in 1864, but the species may have survived in southern Cuba for another twenty years.

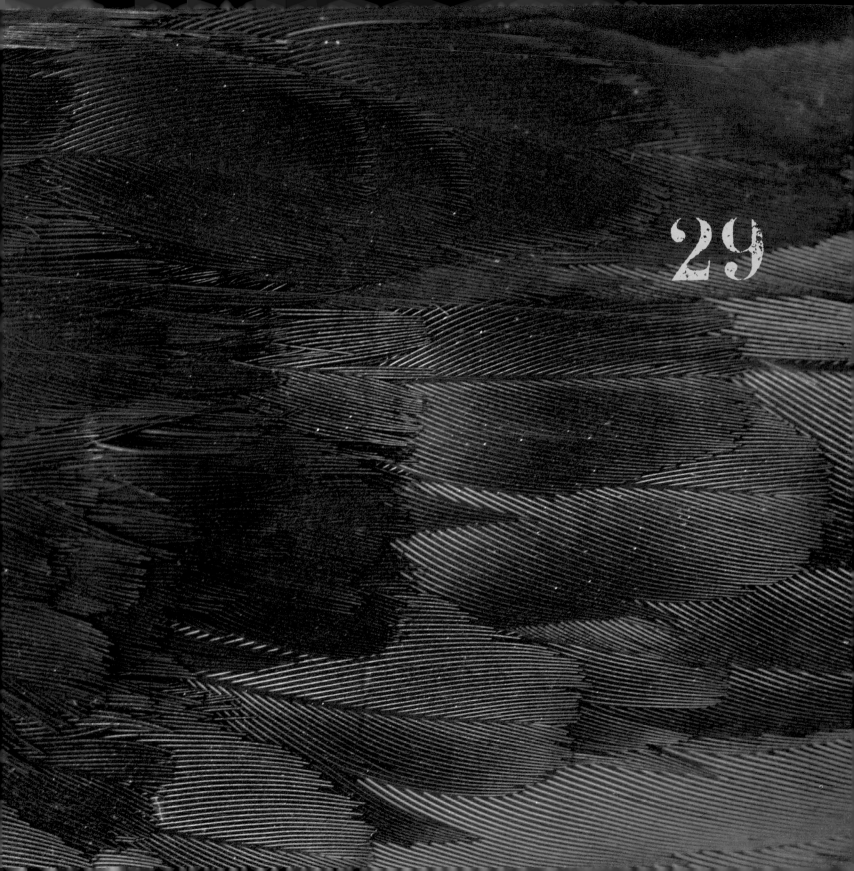

29

EXTINCT
NEW ZEALAND QUAIL

30

Although the New Zealand quail could still be found on the grass-covered downs of South Island in the 1860s, barely fifteen years later it was gone. The loss of this quail, with its intensely colored plumage, is baffling, especially since other species of quail, such as the imported Australian brown quail, were thriving at the same time. Pheasants and quails brought to the island by Europeans as game may have spread disease, and predation by introduced cats and ferrets may have played a role.

{ *Coturnix novaezelandiae* }

DELALANDE'S COUCAL

{ *Coua delalandei* }

Delalande's coucal was a ground-dwelling, nonparasitic cuckoo in Madagascar, the island home of the elephant bird, whose bones are shown here. As with so many of the island's unique inhabitants, the arrival of humans proved fatal to these birds. Certain Malagasy tribes hunted the cuckoo for its lovely blue and green feathers. When Europeans arrived, they brought rats and cats and destroyed the forests. Delalande's coucal became the only cuckoo known to be extinct. A wild bird has not been caught since 1834, although the last sightings date from the 1920s.

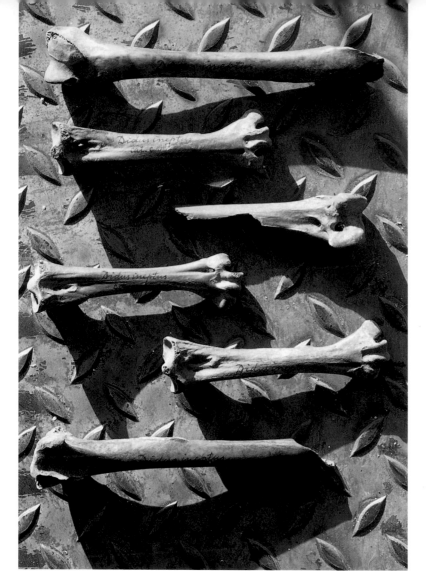

DODO EXTINCT

Little is known for certain about the dodo, a species native to Mauritius, for existing records and drawings are unreliable and contradictory. An ungainly relative of pigeons and doves that had lost the ability to fly, this bird had no predators before Europeans arrived in Mauritius in 1598. Because of its unsavory flavor, the Dutch called the dodo *walghvogel*, or "disgusting bird"; nonetheless, it soon became a source of meat for sailors passing through the Indian Ocean. Nests were plundered by introduced pigs, dogs, and monkeys. A few birds were taken to Europe, and one was exhibited as a curiosity on the streets of London. Fewer than a hundred years after its discovery, the dodo was gone. Bones, a few fragments of skin, the descriptions of amazed travelers, and seventeenth-century illustrations are the only proof that this fantastical bird once lived.

{ *Raphus cucullatus* }

MOA EXTINCT

George Pauley was walking in the Otago area of New Zealand in the 1820s when he encountered a twenty-foot, snake-necked bird. Man and bird both fled in fright. Reports like this were regarded as fiction until 1839, when the famous anatomist Richard Owen announced, on the basis of a single fragment of bone, that New Zealand had once been the home of gigantic flightless birds. Scientists eventually discovered the remains of several species of moa, some the size of chickens and some twelve feet in height. Skin and feathers were still attached, and cut marks on the bones were attributed to iron knives introduced by Europeans, indicating that if moas were extinct, they had disappeared only recently. Maoris claimed that they were still hunting moas in 1770, when Captain Cook first set foot on the islands, and reports of mysterious ostrichlike birds continued into the second half of the nineteenth century.

{ *Emeus crassus* }

{ Hemiphaga novaeseelandiae spadicea }

NORFOLK ISLAND KERERU EXTINCT

The Norfolk Island kereru was first described and last seen in 1801. This large
subspecies of the New Zealand pigeon lived on Norfolk Island, which lies in
the Tasman Sea northwest of New Zealand. Apparently it could not survive the
deforestation and hunting that accompanied the arrival of Europeans. Pigeons
also suffered when New Zealand was colonized, but unlike the population on
Norfolk Island, the New Zealand birds managed to survive. They now appear
to be adapting slowly to the changes in their environment.

Most birds that recently became extinct lived on oceanic islands, where the fragile natural balance is easily disturbed by mammals introduced by humans. Rats have been the most notorious threat, but damage has also been inflicted by cats, dogs, mongooses, goats, and rabbits. Especially hard hit were the rails of the Pacific, many of which had lost their ability to fly as an adaptation to years of island life without predators.

The first specimens of the Hawaiian spotted rail were collected in 1779, during Captain Cook's third voyage, on the big island of Hawaii. Once apparently widespread, this bird was served as a delicacy at the tables of Hawaiian kings. Called *moho* by islanders, meaning "bird that crows in the grass," it lived in open country below the level of the rain forest or in patches of scrub. It was gone by the end of the nineteenth century, its last haunts the sides of the volcano Kilauea and undisturbed areas of the Olaa district.

The small, dark Samoan wood rail was already rare when discovered in 1869 by Johann Kubary, a collector for the Godeffroy Museum in Hamburg. Like other island rails, it fell victim to rats brought by ships. William Pritchard, a former British consul on Fiji, gave an extensive description of the punai, the local name for the bird, noting that it was "excellent eating." Flightless or almost so, the Samoan wood rail had extremely large eyes, which suggests that it was most active at twilight or after dark. A possible sighting was reported in 1988, more than a century after its apparent extinction.

The bar-winged rail was an elusive bird on the Solomon and Fiji islands. Although considered extinct, it may still survive in the inaccessible marshes of Fiji. The bar-winged rail has not been seen since 1890, but in 1973 David Holyoak caught a glimpse of a bird on Viti Levu that fit its description.

HAWAIIAN SPOTTED RAIL

{ *Pennula (Porzana) sandwichensis* } EXTINCT

SAMOAN WOOD RAIL
AND BAR-WINGED RAIL

BOTH PROBABLY EXTINCT

{ *Pareudiastes (Gallinula) pacificus* }
{ *Nesoclopeus poecilopterus* }

EXTINCT

{ *Gallirallus sharpei* } **SHARPE'S RAIL**

This specimen of Sharpe's rail, from the Leiden museum, is the only one in the world. It was purchased in 1865 from the Amsterdam-based natural history dealer G. A. Frank and named for the English ornithologist Richard Sharpe. As is the case for many skins purchased from animal dealers, the origin of this rail is unknown. Over the years curators hoped that new finds would reveal the bird's homeland, yet the mysterious rail was never seen again.

Didus solitarius,

1a, vert. quart (♀?) 1.b. vert. sept? (♂?) 1c, vert. decim.? (♀?) 1d, duodec. (♂?) 2a, pelvis pars. exist. ℔. b. os innomin ℔a, ocas. pars. 3.b. os coracoi ℔4. humerus sinist. ♀. 5. ulna sinist ♂. 6 femur ♀. 7. tibia ♀, 8 fibula ♀. 9. tarsus; ♀. 10. phalanx digit. med. III. phala. prim. dig. interioris. ♀.

pr.p. Prof. Newton, 1868.

35

{ *Pezophaps solitaria* }

EXTINCT RODRIGUEZ SOLITAIRE

In 1691, François Leguat, who fled with some fellow Huguenots to the island of Rodriguez in the Indian Ocean, became enchanted by the flightless local birds. "They walk with such stately form and good grace that one cannot help admiring and loving them," he wrote in 1708. Even the map he drew of the settlement where the refugees lived is decorated with drawings of the Rodriguez solitaire. Yet the Huguenots also praised the birds' excellent taste, particularly when they were young and fat. By the second half of the eighteenth century, passing sailors in search of fresh meat had hunted Leguat's beloved bird to extinction. Like its close relative the dodo, on neighboring Mauritius, the solitaire does not exist as a mounted specimen, but naturalists have pieced together several skeletons from piles of bones found in caves. According to Leguat, when solitaires were caught, they made no sounds but only shed tears.

Mémoires V Sc. natur. T.V.

Brandt Symbolae Sirenologicae

Rhytina borealis Illig.
(Icon idealis.)

W. Pape del.

36

SPECTACLED CORMORANT BOTH EXTINCT
AND STELLER'S SEA COW

{ *Phalacrocorax perspicillatus* }

{ *Hydrodamalis gigas* }

Shipwrecked in 1741 on a gale-swept island in the icy North Pacific, the German naturalist
Georg Steller discovered a large cormorant with rings like spectacles around its eyes.
During his stay on the island, Steller also discovered an immense sea cow. These docile
sirenians, many at least twenty-five feet long, soon became a favorite source of meat for
Steller and his fellow castaways. He wrote: "When one of them was hooked, all the others
were intent upon saving him. Some tried to prevent the wounded comrade from being
drawn on the beach by forming a closed circle around him . . . others laid themselves over
the rope or tried to pull the harpoon out of his body." Hungry Russian hunters and fur
traders slaughtered both the cormorant and the sea cow for their meat. The spectacled
cormorant's clumsy gait and inexperience with humans made it very easy to capture.
Steller's gentle sea cow vanished only twenty-seven years after its discovery, while the
ungainly cormorant survived until the middle of the nineteenth century.

1. AECHMORE.

2. PROSOBONIA LEUCOPTERA
(NATURAL SIZE)

WHITE-WINGED SANDPIPER EXTINCT

{ *Prosobonia leucoptera* }

According to naturalists on board Captain James Cook's ship *Resolution*, this peculiar little shorebird was common over two hundred years ago. Johann Forster, who joined Cook's second voyage in 1773, collected a specimen on Tahiti, and William Anderson, the surgeon on Cook's third expedition, caught two more birds on the island of Moorea in 1777. Two of the birds from these voyages have been lost, but the third, now the only known specimen of a white-winged sandpiper, is in the Leiden museum. Since Cook's voyages there have been no reports of this elegant wader, which was probably a victim of ship rats.

HAWAIIAN O'O EXTINCT

{ *Moho nobilis* }

The intricate ceremonial robes of Hawaiian royalty were made from the brilliant plumage of the royal bird, the o'o. Thousands of these large, confident birds, a species of Hawaiian honeyeater, had to be trapped to get enough feathers to weave the sacred garments. After the choicest yellow feathers had been plucked from tufts beneath the wings, the birds were released, but many did not make it back to the wild. According to S. B. Wilson and A. H. Evans, the authors of an extensive work on Hawaiian birdlife, o'os fried in their own fat were considered a great delicacy. The o'o was still common at the time of Cook's voyages, though the feather trade had been going on for generations, which indicates that disruptions to its habitat brought on by the arrival of Europeans was the cause of extinction. The last Hawaiian o'o was seen in 1934.

{ *Vanellus macropterus* }

JAVANESE WATTLED LAPWING
ENDANGERED

This lapwing, with wattles on its head and long spurs on its wings, once lived in Sumatra, Java, and possibly Timor. In the past, the paddy fields of Java were concentrated on the fertile flanks of the many volcanoes on the island. However, as the human population increased, lowlands were cultivated, and the wet savannas that were home to this striking bird were destroyed. Although the Javanese wattled lapwing is usually categorized as endangered, the last sighting was in East Java in 1939, and it is doubtful that the species survives.

LAUGHING OWL EXTINCT

A hundred years ago, on dark nights, a peculiar laughing cry could be heard over the open rocky country of New Zealand. The mournful song of two laughing owls calling to each other frequently came minutes before rain. These white-faced owls were often languid during the day, which made them easy to capture. They fed on a native rat, the kiore, whose extinction may be the reason for the laughing owl's disappearance by 1914. Sir Walter Buller, a New Zealand ornithologist, recounted the story of a settler in 1905: "It could always be brought from its lurking place in the rocks, after dusk, by the strains of an accordion . . . the bird would silently flit over and face the performer, and finally take up its station in the vicinity, and remain within easy hearing till [the music] had ceased."

{ *Sceloglaux albifacies* }

39

KUSAIE ISLAND STARLING	EXTINCT
{Aplonis corvina}	
PONAPE MOUNTAIN STARLING	ENDANGERED
{Aplonis pelzelni}	
NORFOLK ISLAND STARLING	EXTINCT
{Aplonis fusca hulliana}	
LORD HOWE ISLAND STARLING	EXTINCT
{Aplonis fusca fusca}	

40

Kusaie and Ponape are two of the Caroline Islands, a volcanic archipelago in the West Pacific. During the nineteenth century, Kusaie was popular as a cleaning and repair stop for whalers. At one time the island was said to be completely overrun with rats from these ships. In 1880, Otto Finsch, who later became curator of the bird collection at Leiden, visited Kusaie. He found no trace of the Kusaie Island starling, a solitary bird with a long, curved bill seen on the island fifty years before. On Ponape, the largest island of the Caroline group, Finsch did find the closely related Ponape mountain starling. Last sighted in 1956, this smaller starling may survive today in the island's mountainous forests.

The Norfolk Island and Lord Howe Island starlings are two populations of the same species. The rats responsible for the extinction of the Lord Howe subspecies reached the island when the SS *Makambo* ran aground in June 1918. Until that time the starling was very common and considered a pest by the local fruit farmers. Mysteriously, at the same time the Lord Howe bird disappeared, the Norfolk Island starling vanished from nearby Norfolk Island.

{ Chaunoproctus ferreirostris }

BONIN ISLANDS GROSBEAK

EXTINCT

Kittlitz was the only naturalist to see the Bonin Islands grosbeak alive. He collected several specimens in 1828 when he visited Peel, the largest of the Ogasawara Islands, an archipelago south of Japan formerly known as the Bonin Islands. A report he published in 1832 described the call of the grosbeak as a "soft, pure, high piping note, given sometimes shorter, sometimes longer." Goats, sheep, dogs, and cats that accompanied the settlers who arrived in 1830 probably sealed the fate of the grosbeak, which, like Kittlitz's thrush, was particularly vulnerable because it lived on the ground. The American naturalist William Simpson found no living grosbeaks when he visited Peel Island in 1854.

41

{ Fregilupus varius }

EXTINCT

BOURBON CRESTED
OR RÉUNION ISLAND STARLING

In the early nineteenth century, a Mr. De Cortimoy spent his childhood on Réunion, one of the Mascarene Islands in the Indian Ocean. His letters indicate that he was very familiar with a beautiful ash-gray-and-white starling. He killed dozens of these ground-dwellers with sticks and also kept them in a cage, feeding them bananas, potatoes, and cabbage. After ten years in Paris he returned to Réunion (formerly known as Bourbon), but the Bourbon crested starling had vanished. Although it was extinct by the 1840s, twenty-five museums around the world were able to preserve specimens of this bird.

42

REGILUPUS VARIUS
(NATURAL SIZE)

MOLOKAI KAKAWAHIE
{ *Paroreomyza flammea* }
ENDANGERED

KAUAI AKIALOA
{ *Hemignathus procerus* }
EXTINCT

HAWAII AKIALOA
{ *Hemignathus obscurus* }
EXTINCT

OAHU NUKUPU'U
{ *Heterorhynchus lucidus* }
EXTINCT

MAUI NUKUPU'U
{ *Heterorhynchus affinis* }
ENDANGERED

Human cultivation of the Hawaiian Islands, beginning with the arrival of Polynesians around A.D. 400, has had a disastrous effect on indigenous birds. After Europeans arrived, various rails, thrushes, honeyeaters, and honeycreepers vanished. The Drepanididae family, or Hawaiian honeycreepers, suffered particularly heavy losses. Several species played an important role in pollinating native vegetation, and now many of these plants are also faced with extinction. In place of the vanished birds, volunteers armed with brushes scout the volcanic slopes and carefully transport pollen from one flowering tree to another.

Hawaiian honeycreepers are believed to have evolved from a single ancestor, an American honeycreeper possibly blown to the secluded islands thousands of years ago. Like Darwin's finches of the Galápagos Islands, the honeycreepers developed a variety of amazingly specialized feeding adaptations. Birds that extract honey from flowers or insects from crevices in trees have long, thin, curved beaks, while honeycreepers that live on fruits or seeds have finch- or parrotlike beaks.

Many of the honeycreeper skins in the Leiden museum were donated in 1901 by Alfred Newton, chairman of the joint committee appointed by the Royal Society and British Association for Zoology of the Hawaiian Islands. In an accompanying letter, Newton wrote, "I hope the Birds will be appreciated, as I am sure they will be by you, as you are aware of the fact that the whole indigenous Fauna of the Islands is doomed to extinction, even the insects are rapidly disappearing ('Yes! and even the Landshells!!'). I do not say this to enhance the value of one little collection, but in the interest of science, that all possible care may be taken to keep the specimens for posterity. Of some of these species I am confident it will never be in anybody's power to obtain more specimens."

Newton's pessimism proved justified. By the turn of the century, the mamo, the grosbeak finch, the Oahu nukupu'u, and most forms of the akialoa were extinct. The Kauai akialoa and the Molokai kakawahie were last seen in the 1960s, and although they are listed as endangered, researchers doubt their continued existence. Fewer than thirty of the Maui subspecies of nukupu'u remain.

43

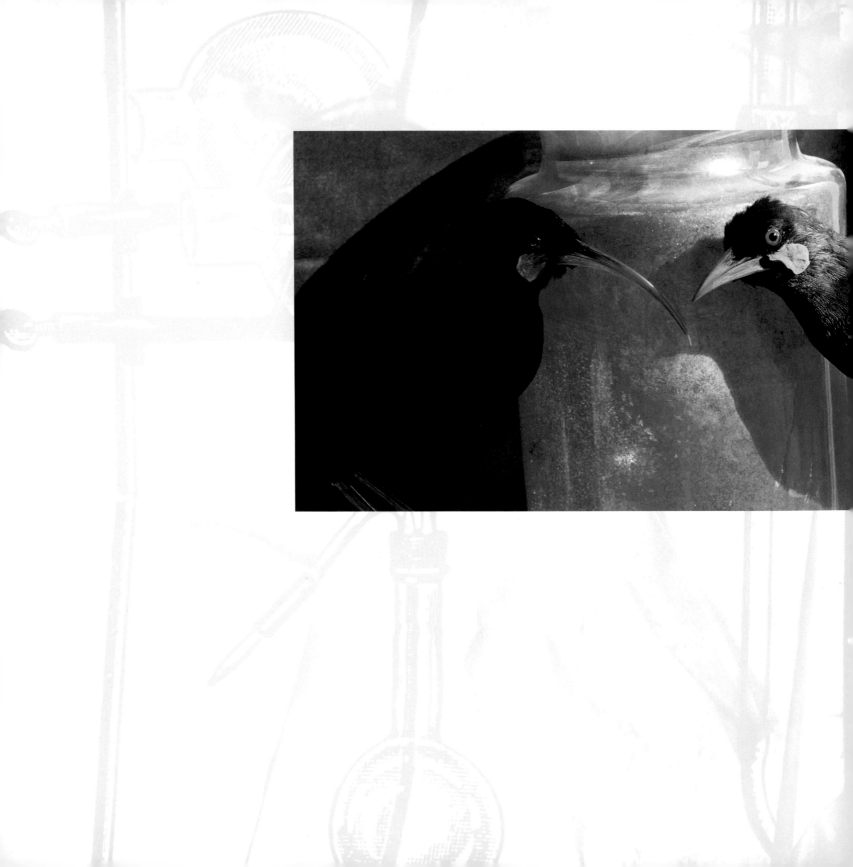

44

EXTINCT **HUIA**

Long before Captain Cook set foot in New Zealand, the Maoris prized the huia for its lovely white-tipped tail feathers, which they wore in battle, gave as tokens of friendship, and used during funeral rites. When huias became scarce, a priest would announce a ban on killing the birds. Europeans ignored these protective taboos, and hunting increased as Maoris followed their careless example. Never widespread, this spectacular black bird began to disappear, a victim of hunting, habitat loss, and diseases brought by birds introduced by Europeans. Collectors valued the huia's striking orange facial wattles and were intrigued that the female's bill was approximately twice as long as the male's. Males used their short bills to drill holes like a woodpecker, while females delicately removed grubs and insects from the bark of trees. The last reliable huia sighting dates from 1907, but reports continued into the 1920s.

{ *Heteralocha acutirostris* }

The greatest threat to island birds has been mammals introduced by humans, especially ship rats, but on Guam birds were faced with an unusual invader: the brown tree snake. So far, nine species or races of birds endemic to Guam have disappeared as a result of the introduction of this reptile. A few of these venomous snakes probably arrived as stowaways on a military ship or plane returning from Southeast Asia to Guam after World War II. One of the snake's victims was the Guam flycatcher. Although it was once common in the forested parts of the island, the species disappeared around 1980.

{ *Myiagra freycineti* }

GUAM FLYCATCHER EXTINCT

45

The inhabitants of Lord Howe, a small island east of Australia, realized over a hundred years ago that ship rats could destroy the balance of life on their island. Vessels were required to drop anchor off the coast and transport cargo in small boats. In spite of these precautions, disaster struck in June 1918. The SS *Makambo* drifted close to shore, and rats invaded Lord Howe. In order to exterminate the rodents, the inhabitants released owls in 1920, but this only made matters worse, since the owls hunted not only rats but many native birds. Alan McCulloch, a Lord Howe resident, wrote in 1921, "Within two years this paradise of birds has become a wilderness, and the quietness of death reigns where all was melody." Ten years after the *Makambo* ran aground, both the Lord Howe thrush and the Lord Howe white-eye had vanished.

{ *Turdus poliocephalus vinitinctus* }

LORD HOWE ISLAND THRUSH EXTINCT
AND LORD HOWE ISLAND WHITE-EYE

{ *Zosterops strenua* }

EXTINCT

46

{ Turnagra capensis }

PIOPIO EXTINCT

When Europeans first reached New Zealand, which they named "Land of Birds," they often wrote of a profound sense of loneliness in the strange landscape. Out of homesickness, they named birds they discovered after familiar species back home; thus a songbird that the Maoris called the piopio also became known as the New Zealand thrush. Extremely curious and even friendly to humans, the piopio would venture into explorers' encampments, seeking scraps. Most vocal in the mornings and after rain, the bird could change its song instantly from a sweet, flutelike melody to a rasping cry. At the time of its discovery in 1773, this lively songbird was common in coastal plains and mountains. Early in the twentieth century it was gone, probably the victim of introduced dogs and cats.

47

BUSH WREN
ENDANGERED

{ *Xenicus longipes* }

The New Zealand wren family comprises four species,
all of which are endangered or extinct. With their short
wings and tails, these minute birds cannot fly far, but
spend their time hopping and darting about the under-
growth. One species, the bush wren, may still survive in
the rugged territory of Fiordland. Another New Zealand
wren, the Stephens Island wren, had its home on a mile-
wide shelf of rock in Cook Strait. This tiny wren, the only
passerine known to have lost the power of flight, had possibly the smallest range of any known bird. The population
was exterminated in 1894 by a single cause: Tibbles,
the lighthouse keeper's cat.

KITTLITZ'S THRUSH
EXTINCT

Before 1827, the entire human population of Peel, the main island of the Ogasawara archipelago, consisted of two castaways. That year the British naval vessel *Blossom* arrived, and barely three years later English, American, and Polynesian immigrants began to settle on the island. The archipelago became a popular repair stop for whaling ships, bringing an invasion of ship rats. Unfortunately, these islands were home to many birds not found elsewhere on earth, including the Bonin Islands grosbeak and Kittlitz's thrush. Because Kittlitz's thrush built its nest on the ground, it was particularly vulnerable to the new predators. American naval expeditions in the 1850s brought the last humans to see this handsome bird alive.

{ *Zoothera terrestris* }

{ *Canis lupus hodophilax* }

Wolves are believed to have migrated from mainland Asia to Japan twice during the ice ages, once to the southern island of Honshu and later to the northern island of Hokkaido. Though both subspecies were much smaller than their European relations, the Honshu wolf, which lived in mountainous woodlands, differed more notably from mainland wolves. Feared and persecuted throughout the rest of the world, wolves were revered in Japan and believed to protect crops from deer. It is still not known why both subspecies vanished in the early twentieth century. This mounted speci-

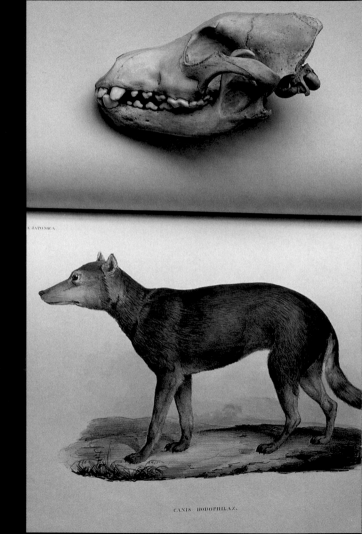

CANIS HODOPHILAX.

HONSHU WOLF EXTINCT

49

EXTINCT
FALKLAND DOG

Neither fox nor wolf, the Falkland dog has mysterious origins. It has been suggested that these gentle creatures descended from an abandoned prehistoric domestic dog. The species survived for thousands of years on a diet of seabirds and seal pups. In 1690 an English captain visiting the barren Falkland Islands discovered the dogs and took one to be his ship's pet, but it was startled by the firing of the ship's cannons and leaped overboard. When Darwin visited the islands in 1833, he feared that the Falkland dog's extreme tameness might lead to its extinction. He was right. Encouraged by a booming market for dog fur, traders lured the trusting animals by holding a piece of meat in one hand and a knife in the other. The final blow came when Scottish farmers, believing that the dogs were killing sheep, organized an intensive poisoning campaign. The last Falkland dog died in 1876 at Shallow Bay, West Falkland.

{ *Dusicyon australis* }

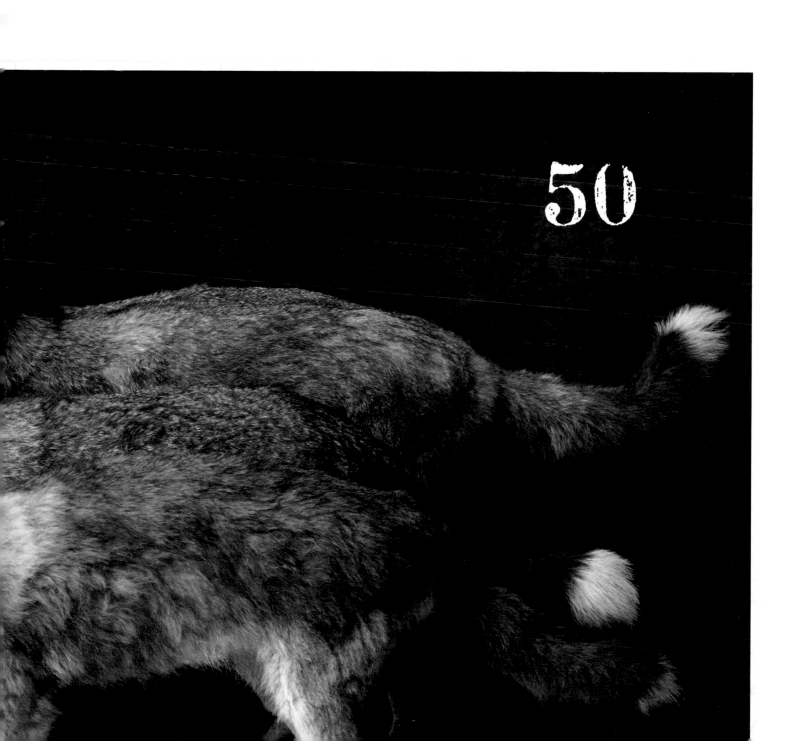

50

{ Megalomys desmarestii }

To prepare the delicate meat of the Martinique giant rice-rat, islanders singed off its hair and exposed its body to air overnight. Then they boiled the rat, using two batches of water to diminish its strong musky odor. Although the rats were heavily hunted, both because they were delicious and because they damaged crops on the island's plantations, they were plentiful and remained on menus at the end of the nineteenth century. A natural disaster caused the animal's extinction. In 1902 the volcano Mount Pelée erupted, and a cloud of poisonous gas not only killed 20,000 islanders but must have wiped out the entire population of the Martinique giant rice-rat, because it was never seen again.

51

EXTINCT
MARTINIQUE GIANT RICE-RAT

JAVAN TIGER EXTINCT

52

{ Panthera tigris sondaica }

Some of the oldest tiger fossils in the world, dating from 1.2 million years ago, have been found on Java. These remains may not be those of a direct ancestor of the Javan tiger. During the ice ages, the larger Indonesian islands were regularly connected to the mainland, and new arrivals replaced the original fauna. Around 50,000 years ago, tigers again reached Java, probably from China. As the sea level rose, the population became isolated and developed into the Javan subspecies, characterized by its dense pattern of stripes. In the early nineteenth century, this tiger was common all over Java. As the human population grew, the tigers were ruthlessly hunted and poisoned, and by 1940 they could be found only in remote mountain ranges and forests. Tigers need a large area with a rich food supply to thrive, and the establishment of game reserves such as Meru Betiri, in rugged eastern Java, came too late to save them. The Javan tiger is thought to have perished by the early 1980s.

EXTINCT **BALI TIGER**

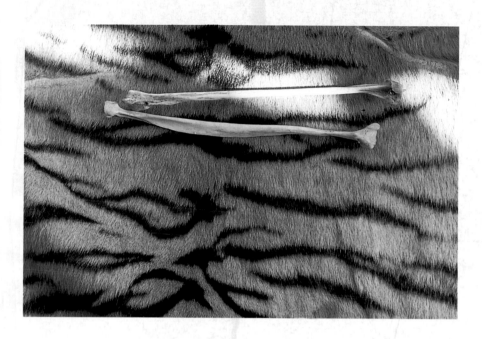

The tiger population of Bali broke off from the Javanese population after the last ice age, when the Bali Strait divided the two islands. Perhaps slightly darker than the Javan tiger, with the same dense pattern of stripes, the Bali tiger was the smallest of all tigers and the one with the easternmost range. As in Java, deforestation drove the tigers to remote mountainous regions. In the early twentieth century, Bali opened its doors and Europeans living in Java organized hunting parties into the western part of the island, decimating the remaining tiger population. The last well-documented Bali tiger died in September 1937, but there were rumors of tigers in northwestern Bali into the early 1950s.

{ *Panthera tigris balica* }

{ Nesolagus netscheri }

ENDANGERED
SUMATRAN HARE

In 1879, the Dutch governor of West Sumatra presented the Leiden museum with a small creature new to science. Although the animal, with short blackish brown ears and a bold pattern of dark brown stripes and patches, looked like a rabbit, it was not closely related to other hares and rabbits. The Sumatran hare lived in dense highland forests. The animals were so shy that local people did not know they existed, although Dutch settlers who owned coffee plantations in the highlands caught them regularly. The last specimen was captured in southern Sumatra in December 1929. Thought to be extinct until photographs of live animals were taken in 1998, the species may still survive in one or more isolated areas, but with the present rate of deforestation, its future seems bleak.

The solenodon, a primitive, shrewlike animal, can move its long, rubbery snout in all directions to reach food deep in the crevices of rocks and trees. With its venomous saliva, it can paralyze its prey — usually insects, worms, small reptiles, and birds — with one bite. Solenodons grow to be a foot long and have stiff, hairless tails of about the same length. They run in an erratic zigzag pattern, and when startled will trip over their toes or tumble head over heels. Active at night, they spend the days in burrows, where females build nests of leaves, grass, and fur and give birth to only a few hairless young. Solenodons were always rare and were presumed extinct before the twentieth century, when two species were rediscovered, first on Hispaniola and later in Cuba. Though they are now protected in forest reserves, they are still threatened by cats, dogs, and mongooses, and their low birthrate makes the populations particularly vulnerable.

SOLENODON ENDANGERED

{ *Solenodon cubanus, Solenodon paradoxus* }

Almiqui — Solenodon paradoxus, Brandt

JAMAICAN GIANT GALLIWASP

A large number of reptiles have disappeared from the West Indies because of introduced cats, dogs, and mongooses. One of these, the Jamaican giant galliwasp, vanished about a century ago. George Shaw wrote of it in 1802, "According to ancient writers the population of Jamaica considered this lizard the most venomous reptile in that island, and that no creature could recover from its bite." Shaw called this "folk superstition" and claimed that the galliwasp was actually harmless. About a foot long, this pale brown lizard had irregular bands of a deeper cast and occasionally turned a vivid golden yellow. It was found in woody and marshy districts, where it fed on fish and fruit. The last of the species probably lived in the Hellshire Hills, a mongoose-free area of the island, where the supposedly extinct Jamaican iguana was recently rediscovered. Whether the Jamaican giant galliwasp has also managed to survive remains to be seen.

CAPE VERDE GIANT SKINK

One of the biggest skinks on record once lived on the inhospitable islands of Razo and Branco in the Cape Verde archipelago, off West Africa. Most skinks are small, agile tropical lizards with shrunken limbs; the larger species are mainly found on islands. Unlike other skinks, the Cape Verde skink, or lagarto, as it was called by locals, was largely vegetarian, feeding on seeds and birds' eggs. Local fishermen prized the giant lizard for its meat. A group of convicts banished to Branco in 1833 lived on fish and lizards, taking a heavy toll on the skink population. Still, the primary cause of extinction was probably a series of severe droughts, which damaged vegetation and caused soil erosion. The last recorded skink in its natural habitat was seen in 1914, when German collectors captured several lizards. According to local people, the lagarto could still be found on the rocky islands until 1940.

RODRIGUEZ GIANT TORTOISE EXTINCT

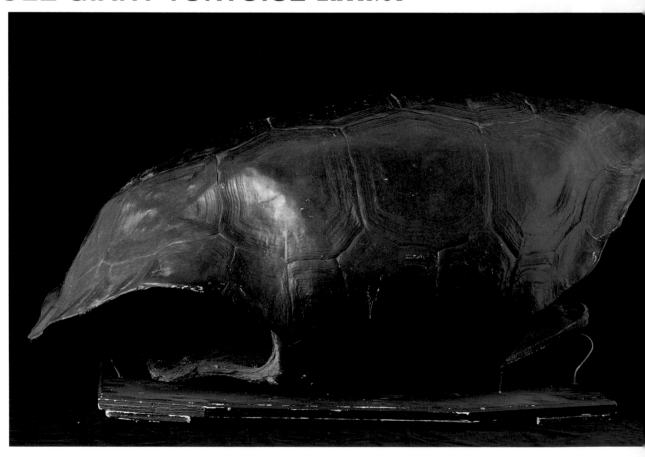

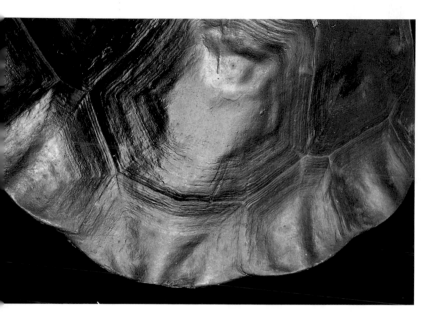

57

{ *Geochelone vosmaeri* }

During the long voyages in the age of sailing ships, tortoises could be kept alive for weeks without food or water, providing a steady supply of fresh meat. Until 1708, the giant tortoises of Rodriguez, one of the Mascarene Islands of the Indian Ocean, were hunted only by a few pirates and the occasional Dutch vessel. In that year the Huguenot refugee François Leguat reported flocks of up to three thousand tortoises on Rodriguez. His journal attracted the attention of the French and British navies and started a dispute over ownership of the "meat supply." Measures to save the animals were unsuccessful. The last of the tortoises on Rodriguez was found at the bottom of a ravine in 1795.

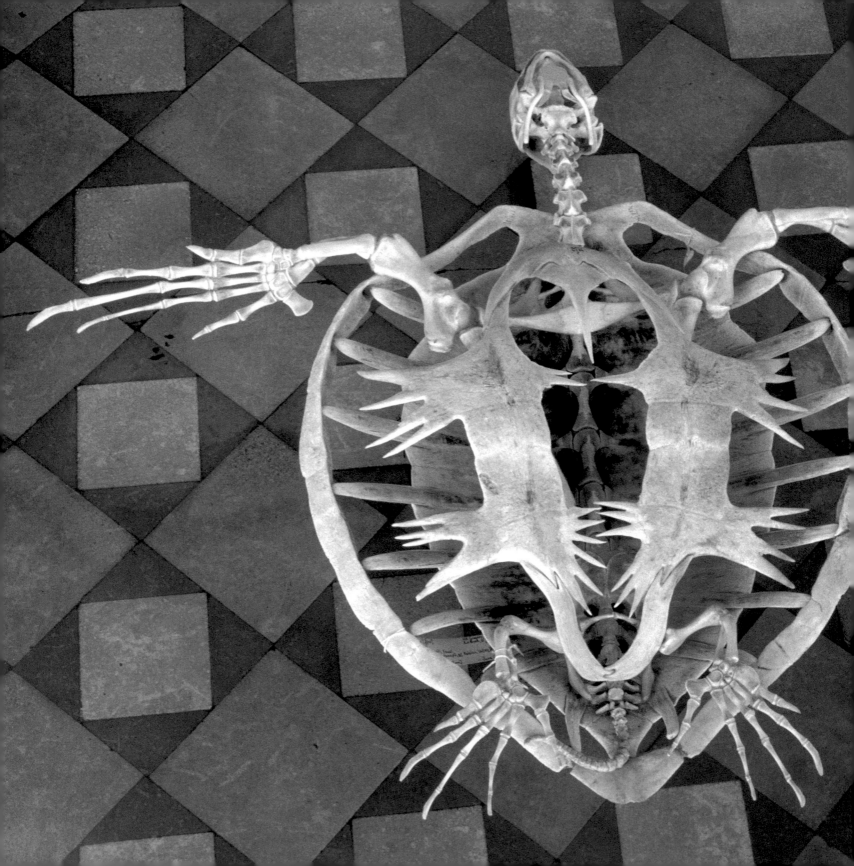

GREEN SEA TURTLE

The green sea turtle is named for its bluish green fat, used to make a delicate broth. The species was once common in shallow areas of the Atlantic, Pacific, and Indian oceans, but many local populations are now in peril. These strong, swift swimmers are awkward on land and leave the water only to lay eggs and bask onshore. Like the giant tortoises of the Galápagos and Mascarene islands, sea turtles could be kept alive for weeks in the holds of sailing ships, providing valuable fresh meat before the invention of refrigeration. More recently, hunters sought turtle oil to make cosmetics and turtle skin for the leather trade. Females were turned on their backs as they came onto the beach and slaughtered before they could lay their eggs. Egg collection was also detrimental to the plummeting population. International conservation efforts now include strict control of the trade in sea turtle products, the protection of nesting beaches, and the establishment of hatcheries.

{ *Chelonia mydas* }

{*Achatinella* and *Carelia* spp.}

HAWAIIAN LAND SNAILS

From the 1850s until the early 1900s, Europeans in Hawaii gathered vast shell collections. For example, the collector J. T. Gulick accumulated 44,500 snail shells in three years. He reported riding with ten others into a valley in 1853 and returning by four in the afternoon with more than 1,400 snails. In 1887, D. D. Baldwin wrote of picking snails "from trees and low bushes as rapidly as one would gather huckleberries." Overcollecting may have been one factor in the disappearance of the lovely multicolored snails that once covered the trees of the islands, but devastating habitat destruction began when prehistoric Polynesian settlers cleared lowland vegetation for farming. Europeans, arriving in the 1800s, destroyed more habitat and introduced predatory rats. Currently, the most serious threat is *Euglandina rosea*, a carnivorous snail that was brought to Hawaii to control the introduced giant African land snail but that also attacks tree snails and other snails unique to the islands. More than half of Hawaii's terrestrial snails are extinct. The largest, showiest tree snails, species of the genus *Achatinella*, are on the federal endangered species list.

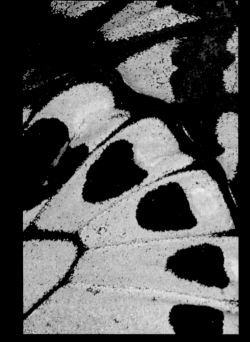

BIRDWING BUTTERFLIES ENDANGERED

Birdwings, a genus of elusive lepidopterans from islands in the Pacific Ocean, are the largest butterflies in the world. All species of birdwings are brilliantly colored, but they vary in patterning and detail from region to region, and females are always less showy than males. They are highly prized by collectors, and many species are very rare and usually seen only in museums and collectors' cabinets. Although protected by law, birdwings are continually threatened by the destruction of their rain forest habitats. Queen Alexandra's birdwing (*Ornithoptera alexandrae*), of Papua New Guinea, is the largest, with a wingspan of up to one foot. Its native environment is increasingly threatened by ever-spreading plantations. The nineteenth-century biologist and explorer Alfred Wallace described catching a birdwing: "I had taken it out of the net and was gazing, lost in admiration, at the velvet black and brilliant green of its wings, seven inches across, its golden body, and crimson breast . . . I had seen similar insects in cabinets at home, but it is quite another thing to capture such one's self . . . to gaze upon its fresh and living beauty, a bright gem shining out amid the silent gloom of a dark and tangled forest."

{ *Ornithoptera* spp. }

The aye-aye of Madagascar is so unusual-looking that Europeans initially thought it was a squirrel, and it was not classified as a primate until about 1800. This solitary, nocturnal creature is the size of a house cat and has a bushy tail and huge orange owl-like eyes. It listens for grubs beneath the bark of trees, then tears into the bark with its chisel-shaped front teeth and uses its elongated, skeletal middle finger to extract the larvae. It also uses this twiglike middle finger to scoop out the juice and meat of coconuts and other fruit. Habitat destruction continues to threaten the scattered population, and in some areas villagers believe the aye-aye is a harbinger of disaster and kill it on sight. It is said that if an aye-aye points its long, bony middle finger at someone, that person will die a swift, unpleasant death.

{ *Daubentonia madagascariensis* }

AYE-AYE ENDANGERED

61

62

{ *Propithecus verrauxi coquereli* }

COQUEREL'S SIFAKA

ENDANGERED

Coquerel's sifaka, with its blazing yellow eyes and masklike face, can be distinguished from other sifakas by an all-white head and maroon chest, shoulders, and thighs. Weighing around eight pounds as an adult and covered with thick body hair, this lemur is threatened by forest destruction and is now restricted almost entirely to the Ankarafantsika and Bora nature reserves in northwestern Madagascar. Sifakas, named for their loud *si-fak* calls, are spectacular arboreal acrobats. Their hind limbs have evolved to be much longer than their forelimbs, so they can cling and jump effortlessly. They may cover distances of up to thirty feet in one leap, using their long tails to help balance and steer.

NORFOLK ISLAND KAKA

63

The last Norfolk Island kaka is said to have died in a cage in London in 1851. However, this large parrot may have survived into the second half of the nineteenth century on nearby Philip Island, where it was hunted by settlers and convicts for its meat. The Norfolk Island kaka had a cry that sounded like a dog's barking in the treetops, and although it resembled its close relative the New Zealand kaka, the Norfolk Island breed was very shy. Several specimens had deformed, elongated bills, causing one naturalist to mistakenly declare them a totally new species of parrot in 1860.

{ *Nestor productus* }

The last breeding colony of the Japanese sea lion, which looked very much like its better-known relative the California sea lion, was found on the small rocky island of Takeshima, which was occupied by Korea after World War II. There are rumors that during the war Korean soldiers used these animals for target practice. Though data on the sea lion have long been unavailable, this little-known subspecies may have vanished forever. Sea lions in Japanese waters in the 1960s were probably California sea lions that had escaped from zoos. Colonies spotted by Japanese fishermen on the precipitous cliffs of Korea's eastern coast are most likely Steller's sea lions.

{ *Zalophus californianus japonicus* }

EXTINCT

JAPANESE SEA LION

64

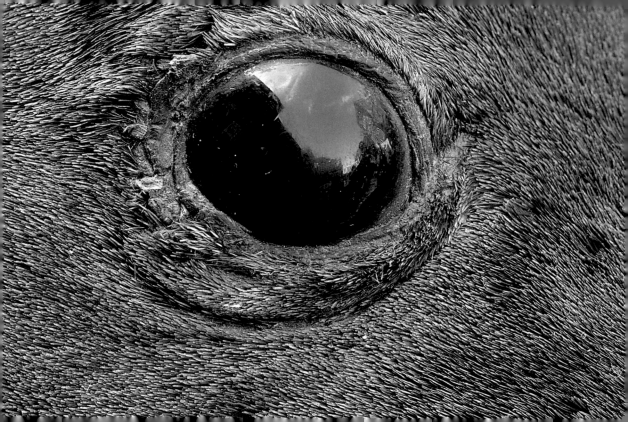

EXTINCT

WEST INDIAN MONK SEAL

65

{ *Monachus tropicalis* }

For millions of years, swarms of monk seals rested and gave birth on the sandy beaches of islands in the Pacific, the Mediterranean, and the Caribbean. Monk seals, distinguished by the cowl-like fold of fat on their necks, are the most ancient of seals. These "living fossils" are gentle, which makes them easy to exploit, and their breeding areas are extremely vulnerable to disruption. West Indian monk seals appear in the account of Columbus's second voyage to America and in 1494 received the dubious honor of being the first New World mammal killed by the explorer. After Columbus, fishermen, who saw the seals as competition, and sealers clubbed them to death in great numbers. They disappeared from their last stronghold, a group of coral islands called Serranilla Bank, shortly after 1952. Two species of monk seal live in the Atlantic, the Mediterranean, and in the waters of the Hawaiian archipelago, but both are in danger of following the path of their Caribbean relations.

ROSS D. E. MacPHEE, Ph.D.

Curator and Chairman, Department of Mammalogy,
American Museum of Natural History

REMEMBER THE ISLANDS

The continents are the world's chief biotic reservoirs, the places where most of the planet's plants and animals are found. And so it is assumed that the looming crisis in biodiversity — the threat that tens of thousands of species will disappear in the next century or so, unless we are able to prevent it — will be decided by what happens to continental floras and faunas. Whether there is still time to avert this catastrophe, and what form it may eventually take, are unknown. But as *Swift as a Shadow* shows in ample detail, we have already had a sampling of what the future may hold. In particular, island extinctions reveal that the biodiversity crisis is not a theoretical notion: for the world's islands, this crisis has largely come and gone.

For some groups, such as birds, almost all extinctions known to have occurred in recent times have taken place on islands. ("Recent times" and "modern era" are usefully vague expressions that I use to refer in a general way to the past thousand years, with an emphasis on the last four centuries.) This holds true as well for mollusks, mammals, reptiles, some other animals, and flora. While the general causes of extinctions on islands are not necessarily different from those on mainlands, the small size of most islands means that single causes can have unusually dramatic effects.

Island flora and fauna are frequently described as "impoverished." Typically, species numbers are low and there are few major evolutionary lineages, because island resources tend to be severely restricted, limiting the numbers and kinds of species that can be supported. But as Alfred Russel Wallace and Charles Darwin were the first to recognize in the nineteenth century, in the midst of this apparent poverty the confining circumstances of island life create fertile opportunities for natural selection. The development of partial or complete flightlessness in some rails, marine adaptations in some lizards, and dwarfism in elephants are just a few of the specializations that have appeared in island-dwelling members of these groups but are rarely, if ever, seen in their continental cousins. Some of these adaptations obviously evolved to enable species to utilize resources that were previously unavailable to them; in other cases, we can only guess at the basis for the adaptation.

Specialization for island life may carry with it hidden costs — costs that can become unbearably high if conditions change. A rail or pigeon flock that has recently arrived on a small island may be faced with very limited options for survival if the potential food supply is poor or seasonal. One way of solving the problem might be to increase average body size, which would enable the species to rely on foods that are low in nutrients but can be stored as fat. Since increased body size in birds often precludes flight, we can think of flightlessness as the price these birds pay to adapt and survive on an island with few amenities. The cost is low as long as there are no predators or competitors; once these appear, however, the debt is open for collection. And on most of the world's islands, the price has been ferociously high.

If every tragedy contains a lesson for those willing to explore it, what can we learn from island losses? Exactly how large have they been, and what factors have played the greatest roles? What does the fate of island biotas portend for areas other than islands? Let's concentrate here on disappearances among vertebrates, especially birds and mammals.

Establishing how many species have been lost on islands during recent times requires more analysis than a simple body count. According to one deliberately cautious appraisal by the World Conservation Monitoring Centre (WCMC), in the last four centuries there have been at least 116 losses of birds at the full species level. ("Full species" means that the species in question differs in some definite, heritable way from every other species, so that it can be uniquely identified and counted.) I should, however, underscore that conservation biologists recognize the importance of preserving distinct populations within portions of species' ranges. Although a species is considered extant as long as at least one of its populations remains viable, substantial loss of subspecies reduces a species' genetic endowment, which in the long run is an invitation to disaster. Losses at the subspecies level may therefore be said to differ only in magnitude from complete extinction at the species level — and in this book both levels are highlighted.

In a recent study, my colleague Clare Flemming and I estimated that approximately eighty-eight full species of mammals have been lost around the world in the past five hundred years. This figure suggests that in relatively recent times, mammalian losses have been about 25 percent fewer than bird losses. However, these figures are based on "verified" losses: only named species, based on physical specimens, have been included in the tallies. Ornithologist David Steadman has recently challenged the verified-losses concept as applied to birds, claiming that it greatly underestimates the number of recent avian extinctions, most of which have occurred on the myriad small islands of the Pacific. He believes that the real figure for bird losses in the past eight centuries or so may exceed *two thousand* species, only a handful of which have ever been recovered in the form of bones or other remains. If he is correct — and the inferential evidence is certainly on his side — then almost one fifth of *all* Holocene bird species have vanished, the great majority of them within the past five hundred to eight hundred years. According to the WCMC, at least 90 percent of all recent avian extinctions occurred on islands; if we use Steadman's figures, the number may exceed 99 percent. By contrast, consider the data for Asia: during the modern era, this vast continent may have lost only three bird species, compared to at least thirteen for the Hawaiian Islands alone!

Except for bats, mammals have a poor record of colonization of distant oceanic islands. Rafting on an accommodating piece of vegetation is one of the few ways that mammals can reach and colonize islands, and the chances for success are vanishingly small. Thus it is improbable that there is a still undiscovered mammalian counterpart to the catastrophic bird losses in the central Pacific. But other vertebrates living on islands have suffered disproportionately high rates of extinction, indicating that this phenomenon is hardly limited to birds and mammals. For example, twenty-three reptile species are verified as extinct on the WCMC list (probably a serious underestimate), and fully some twenty-two of them are island species.

Although freshwater fish exist on true islands, what is much more striking is the enormous numbers of species that live in continental habitats that are just as isolated — and just as threatened — as any island. For example, in the past two decades, Lake Victoria has lost more than two hundred native species of haplochromine cichlids because of overfishing and the introduction of an exotic predator, the Nile perch. Similar massive reductions, running to hundreds of species in all, have been catalogued for the freshwater fish of Malaysia, West Africa, Mexico, and Andean lakes. Karst ponds, mountain lakes, and rivers that drain to inland basins may not be true islands, but in evolutionary and ecological terms they often function as though they were, with all the attendant possibilities and costs.

The death of a species is usually said to be marked by the loss of its last individuals. More properly, however, it is marked by the last successful reproductive act: once the genetic material that defines a species is no longer in a position to reproduce itself, that species is terminal. This can happen if no reproductively competent adults are available, or if there are so few of them that they have little chance of encountering one another and mating. The vicissitudes of island life suggest another important factor. Other things being equal, a large population well distributed in an area has a hedge against extinction: even if many individuals die in a sudden catastrophe, they will eventually be replaced by individuals from elsewhere in the species' range. Island vertebrates are thus at risk, practically by definition. Their confined distribution and small population sizes are part of the adaptive bargain struck by their more generalized ancestors. Sacrificed in this deal were flexibility and resiliency; any catastrophe that substantially reduces the current population of an island species may simply be fatal, because there is no source of replenishment.*

If approximately eighty-eight species of mammals have been lost since 1500, that is a considerable number — roughly seventeen species per century. However, humans have been affecting the world for a much longer time. How many extinctions occurred before the modern era, and how were they caused? Although there is uncertainty in making such estimates, by my count we know of approximately 350 species of mammals that have died out in the past 60,000 years, on both continents and islands. (This date is important, for it marks the point at which we have the first definitive evidence of anatomically modern humans outside their home continents of Africa and Eurasia.) About 80 percent of these late Quaternary losses occurred before 1500 —

a rate of one extinction every two hundred years, which may seem fairly low. But this masks a critical fact: in the majority of well-dated cases, these ancient extinctions were highly localized in time and space. They occurred in the form of short, sharp bursts, in single regions or landmasses, often involving substantial losses in shockingly brief periods of time. The feature that binds these events together is that they occurred directly after initial human settlement. For this reason, I call them "first-contact extinctions."

Three other features of first-contact extinctions are important to note. First, after the initial catastrophic loss in an area, extinction rates tended to drop markedly, and they remained low until the modern era (when they sometimes heated up again, as in the case of Australia). Thus, in the Americas, 135 mammal species were lost around 11,000 years ago, within a millennium or so of initial human arrival from Asia via the Bering land bridge. In the following 10,000 years, only three mammal species have become verifiably extinct in the New World exclusive of the West Indies (although once again it is important to emphasize that many distinct populations or subspecies have disappeared within this period).

Second, species of large body size (so-called megafaunal species, or ones weighing more than 50 kilograms) were

---

* Isolation can also be a form of protection. In a few cases, island-bound populations of mainly continental species have managed to persist long after their mainland relatives have been driven to extinction. Classic examples are the bettongs and hare-wallabies of Dorre and Bernier Islands in Shark Bay, off the coast of western Australia. Mainland populations were lost to introduced species, habitat destruction, and possibly disease; the islands have managed to avoid these impacts — so far — and have therefore kept their resident marsupials. But it doesn't take much imagination to see that their tenure is precarious.

more seriously affected than smaller species. In the case of the extinctions in the Americas 11,000 years ago, the ratio of loss of large mammals to small ones was four to one. In Madagascar, 80 percent of megafaunal vertebrates died out within a millennium or so of human arrival about two thousand years ago. In the West Indies, all mammals larger than 50 kilograms (sloths and very large rodents) and many large raptors have died out since human colonization began about seven thousand years ago, and many smaller ones have disappeared as well. By contrast, on a global basis, only one in six mammal extinctions since 1500 has been in the megafaunal range. (This change in ratios may be partly due to the fact that so many large species are gone, but it cannot be the whole story.)

The third feature seems almost paradoxical. Two areas of the globe have been spared massive extinctions of mammals in recent times, and — incredibly — they are Africa and Eurasia, the lands of oldest human residency. The paleontological record is good enough to establish that dramatic pulses of extinction have not occurred on these continents at any point during the last 60,000 years or more. Further, the handful that actually took place were not concentrated in time, as they were elsewhere.

Some consider all three features to be related. Paul Martin, of the University of Arizona, has suggested that the low rate of extinction in Africa and Eurasia has to do with behavioral evolution. Because African and Eurasian megafaunal species evolved in the same geographical and ecological contexts as our early ancestors, they had time to develop anti-predator defenses against modern humans. Species in other parts of the world, faced with sudden human arrival, had no time to develop such defenses and therefore rapidly succumbed. Succumbed to what? Martin suggests overhunting, and certainly this kind of direct impact has been implicated in a number of modern-era extinctions. However, it has proven remarkably hard to demonstrate this factor at work in ancient extinctions. For example, it is widely accepted that hunting pressure was the primary cause of extinction of the moa in New Zealand eight hundred years ago. This interpretation is supported by evidence in the form of numerous kill sites, moa refuse in occupation sites, worked moa bone, and so forth. By contrast, such indicators of direct human impact are missing in the case of the loss of the elephant birds of Madagascar at about the same time: there are no sites of mass mortality, elephant birds never turn up in archaeological sites (although their eggs occasionally do), and nothing ever seems to have been fashioned from their bones. Were the early Malagasy simply not interested in hunting?

With no good evidence of overhunting, it has been suggested that perhaps habitat destruction — deforestation through burning — was the leading cause of extinction in Madagascar. However, as paleoecologist David Burney has shown, the deforestation argument has been seriously overblown; there is in fact very little evidence that the interior of Madagascar was significantly forested at any time within the past two or three thousand years. There is not much else we can point to in the litany of causes that have apparently provoked extinctions elsewhere. Archaeologist Bob Dewar has pondered whether cattle and cattle-herding could have precipitated some extinctions, and has concluded that there is no solid supporting evidence. Two dozen species of native vertebrates died out nonetheless.

In my view, one other possible cause of extinctions on islands has been undervalued in the past: infectious diseases. Disease can explain why Afro-Eurasian mammals suffered fewer extinctions (they shared the same disease pool with humans), why megafaunal species suffered disproportionately (large species have lower reproductive rates; disease affects the very old and the very young), and why extinction rates characteristically drop after first contact (surviving species have gained genetic immunity through severe selection pressure). And it isn't necessary to infer that technologically unsophisticated peoples were particularly prone to killing or destroying habitat, which has always seemed to me quite improbable and at odds with the view of human ecologists that primitive peoples tend to be in tune with their environments.

Naturally, there are problems with the disease theory as well. The most serious one is that we have never identified any disease that could jump from species to species at the rate that would be necessary to cause, for example, the diverse losses of mammals, birds, and reptiles in Madagascar a thousand years ago. And there is no conclusive evidence that diseases have caused the complete extinction of any species except for one land snail, the entire population of which consisted of a half-dozen captive individuals at the time of extinction. Disease has been strongly implicated in a few other cases. One concerns the honeycreepers of Hawaii, some species of which may have declined to extinction after the introduction of the mosquito (*Culex quinquefasciatus*) that carries avian malaria. Experiments with surviving honeycreeper species (which are restricted to mountain flanks above the limit of mosquito distribution) indicate that these birds are highly susceptible to avian malaria. Two more examples come from Christmas Island, which lies between Indonesia and Australia. Apparently this island was missed by oceangoing humans until the nineteenth century. It supported two native rats, described by the British Museum biologist Charles Andrews as being exceedingly common in 1897, just after humans began to settle there permanently. When Andrews returned to Christmas Island a decade later, he was astounded to discover that the rats were gone. He learned that a few years before, the rats, one of which was nocturnal, suddenly appeared in droves in broad daylight, acting erratically, as though they were ill. Then they were seen no more. Andrews suggested that an epidemic brought in by ship rats could have caused the extinction. Alas, no one knows.

The common thread in my examples is that these massive extinctions do not occur until the first arrival of humans and their fellow travelers (including domesticated animals and pets and the parasites and pathogens that live on or in them). Mere correlation does not, of course, mean that introduced diseases necessarily caused or even contributed to these extinctions. But it is a possibility — one that several researchers are now investigating. Real proof that diseases can cause extinctions would have revolutionary implications.

Humans and introduced pathogens are not the only exotic species we should worry about. Species that are not native to an area are the biological equivalent of wild cards in a poker game. In one situation they may have no obvious effect, but in another they may seriously disrupt delicate ecological balances. And as in a game of chance, outcomes are often unpredictable for all players. Humans may be the ultimate destructive exotic, but there are many other examples. A particularly chilling one is the brown tree snake, accidentally introduced into Guam a few decades ago. This snake is a voracious eater, and it is estimated that it has caused or contributed to the extinction of nine species or subspecies of native Guamanian birds.

A final point concerns habitat availability and species numbers. One of the clearest facts of natural history is the connection between the size of a given area and the number of species it can support. It follows from this relationship that any reduction of area will also mean a reduction in the number of species supported. And in fact there is ample evidence for this.

Scientists have been particularly concerned that forest fragmentation — disappearance of forest caused by clear-cutting, land clearing for monoculture, urbanization, road-building, and so forth — will result in waves of extinction in the future, because the fragments will not be able to support all of the species that the intact forest sustained. In Brazil, scientists have tried to document the disappearance of bird species in the Atlantic coastal lowland forest, one of the most devastated forests in the world. Once cloaking much of the southeastern part of the country, this forest has been reduced to a fraction (12 percent) of its size only a century ago — and this reduction shows. A number of native birds are confined to small areas within the remnants of this forest, and it is predicted that if current deforestation rates continue, a large number of currently threatened species (60 out of a total of 214 native bird species) could quickly become extinct.

Another problem with cutting tropical forests into a series of small plots separated by open expanses or secondary growth is that the forest quickly ceases to function as *humid* forest. Continuous humid forest in the topics is wet not only because it rains a lot but because the evaporation rate is low under dense canopies. In order to thrive, many forest invertebrates must have conditions of high relative humidity. Cutting down forest exposes the remnants to the effects of wind and sun and thereby to the loss of moisture. In effect, the edge of a forest plot becomes proportionately larger as the plot's area decreases, and this "edge effect" is especially hazardous for biodiversity.

These examples illustrate the point that forest fragments are in effect virtual islands. Many of the problems of small size, isolation, and limited resources found in the world's islands occur in virtual islands as well. For animals that cannot adapt to their changed circumstances, the consequence will very likely be local extirpation or even outright extinction. As we have seen — and as this book so poignantly depicts — the fate of island fauna over the millennia shows all too clearly that this threat is terribly real. When next you contemplate the fate of the world's forests, remember the islands.

ROSAMOND PURCELL

NATURE STANDS ASIDE

The museum has its methods, but with all due respect, the system often has a way of closing out the cosmos from which each creature came. The urgent need, as ecosystems collapse, for scientists to gather statistics on each animal — natural history, geographical range, and conservation status — tends to make the ode, the painting, the prayer, seem extraneous. Scientific data are attached to bull and butterfly alike, but there is not enough room on the card or in the catalogue to report how the philosopher, the villager, the forest dweller, or the poet saw the animal walk, crawl, zigzag, or soar.

This roll call on paper of Leiden's extinct and endangered animals and birds has been supplemented by a few rare specimens from other museums. And yes, they are all, obviously, dead — but how these dead can dance! Although life passes, patterns and forms remain, and there is nothing like bringing beautiful feathers, bones, and fur to the light of day. In the grassland of New Zealand, the quail flew up in seconds. In the museum, the same quail are motionless, but the light is always moving — and daylight, changing minute by minute and hour by hour as it falls across the feathers, reanimates the birds. The effect of feathers, bones, scales, or horn bathed in light and the study of seasonal changes in the quality of light are crucial to this, my style of photography.

The visual potential of these organic remains should not be separated from their biological and historical significance. But the subject of this book is also the ethos of the archives. As a sojourner, I relish the random search: wandering through miles of corridors, opening hundreds of heavy doors, and choking through fumes, dust, and dark to find the holy grail. To work here requires an invitation. In 1995, when several members of the curatorial staff of the National Museum of Natural History in Leiden invited me to photograph their extraordinary collection, I felt that thrill that comes with unexpected privilege. For many years, off and on, other curators have said, "No, you may not handle that animal, it is a type specimen, it is unique." Entering these archives with this assignment, I felt as though I had been trusted to leaf through the Gutenberg Bible.

Science may classify, but art rearranges. Visually speaking, a group mitigates the horror: one bird is a dead bird; a pile of birds becomes an event. As the colors blend and cross, the museum — not nature — displays its bounty.

Whatever their scientific status may be, the animals and birds are captive specimens, and they often bear the scars of human divisiveness on their skins and bones. There are signs of a campsite's fire on moa bones, and an arrogant label, "dido ineptus," on the dodo. I have examined many taxidermied stitches, seen straw, metal, and cotton poking through the skins — to say nothing of the bullet holes, amputation marks, metal hooks, and bolts, many postmortem features shared by quagga and common crow alike.

The prosimians and other primates in the Leiden museum have always fascinated me. Their prepared faces, with or without teeth, are fixed in perpetual gormlessness or bared-teeth smiles of sweet mischief or rage. Forearms grasp fake tree limbs or pale yellow posts, while the smaller monkeys either threaten with clenched fists or beg with upturned leathery palms, theatrical poses that further emphasize the artificiality of this mostly eighteenth- and nineteenth-century collection.

From the beginning, the museum in Leiden retained groups of preparators to work on the animals and birds, which came both from expeditions and from zoos. Stuffed with cotton, straw, and peat moss (the least durable, the least expensive) taken from Dutch bogs, the animals acquired facial expressions and gestures through the imagination of the taxidermist, who most likely had not been in the field. Some postures, while plausible, are not appropriate to the particular animal. The suppliant gesture of the outstretched hand of the monk saki or the squirrel monkey may well have come from firsthand observation of a live macaque from Java, visible on the streets of Leiden as the organ grinder's begging partner.

Creatures preserved in alcohol and formalin float up through a yellowing viscous veil. The preservation of the skins and feathers requires dim closets and plenty of PDB (para-dichlorobenzene). Sometimes a trace of the desperate animal smell will rise up through the chemicals; occasionally I believe I catch a whiff of true fur, of a particular final moment of life, the rank scent of fear. But sounds — there are none.

Many of these animals were well documented in the field and as specimens have a venerable past. The dramas accompanying their fates range from low-key to swashbuckling, full of intrigue. In the late eighteenth century, for example, the French invaded Holland and carried off as part of their loot many natural history specimens. In 1815, Dr. Brugmans, an enterprising envoy, rode to Paris to bring the treasures back. The French, both unwilling to return and unable to find much of what they had taken, gave back this and that, and in so doing divested themselves of some of their own valuable type-specimens (and of at least one pet monkey belonging to a well-placed demoiselle). Some of the Dutch specimens are in Paris still.

The specimens in Leiden survived the bombs of World War II and were until 1998 entirely housed in a many-storied building with open-grid steel floors that contribute to the visitor's sense of vertigo — a vertigo engendered by the sheer quantity of stuff. "Do you have a kiwi?" I asked once, and I was shown more than forty exquisite mounts, not to mention piles of skins and boxes of bones. Kiwis? Snow leopards? Dugongs? Jerboa? Just ask, and then struggle with the evidence. I have been told that there are up to 11 million specimens in this place, and that each jar filled with such preciousness as a hundred tiny shrimp or land snails counts as a single entry.

Just because the remains of rare animals are stored in museums doesn't mean they are secure. A specimen without provenance — or, worse, without the multidigit number assigned by the institution — assumes an endangered state within the archives, however classified in the wild. (Lack of subscription functions as a fatal illness does in a living animal.) The significance of a specimen in the context of any collection is determined almost entirely by the degree of accompanying data: field notes, date of capture, collector, place of origin, scientifically accurate drawings. In a given collection there may be two hundred skins of passenger pigeons with no data and two common birds captured by a brilliant naturalist who gave them to an illustrious king with the gilt-edged papers to prove it all. Who is to say where true value lies?

As the photographer contemplating all the spoils, I bring further baggage to the event; which of these pigeons, say, will look "best" on film? In the middle of my contemplation of the Berber lion, a technician came by to reglue the painted tongue as naturally as a Hollywood makeup artist would mend a monster mask. Several wallabies and a wolf were also carefully vacuumed, the quagga long ago cleaned. In one of the photographs, the reflected glass case in which one New Zealand quail is displayed creates a shadow enclosure for the second. The kereru dive-bombs into its own box, set on red velvet. This is artificial, you might say — and I say that this is an almost thoroughly artificial situation. This is a warehouse full of valuable clues, not only to the nature of predators and prey but to the venerable history of artifice — of velvet, paint, plaster fruit, maquettes of string and cotton, iron hooks for hanging birds to dry.

Bracing my tripod, I can look down through four floors of airy caging; I stand inside a giant ribbed animal surrounded by multitudes in a silent place. As is my custom, I use only daylight for this photography, and because the Dutch believe in building windows that reach from floor to ceiling, there is almost always daylight here. In other ways, it must be said that in this place, nature stands aside.

Naphthalene crystals, long used by natural history museums to disinfect skins in their collections.

REFERENCES AND SUGGESTED READING

Baillie, Jonathan, and Brian Groombridge, eds. *1996 IUCN Red List of Threatened Animals*. Gland, Switzerland: IUCN (World Conservation Union), 1996.

Earle, Sylvia. *Sea Change: A Message of the Oceans*. New York: Putnam, 1993.

Ferguson-Lees, James, and Emma Faull. *Endangered Birds*. London: George Philip, 1987.

Fuller, Errol. *Extinct Birds.* London: Viking/Rainbird, 1987.

———. *The Great Auk.* Southborough, England: privately published, 1999.

Jolly, Alison. *A World Like Our Own: Man and Nature in Madagascar*. New Haven, Conn.: Yale University Press, 1980.

MacPhee, Ross D. E., ed. *Extinctions in Near Time: Contexts, Causes, and Consequences*. New York: Plenum, 1999.

Mann, Charles, and Mark Plummer. *Noah's Choice: The Future of Endangered Species*. New York: Knopf, 1995.

Mittermeier, Russell A., Ian Tattersall, William R. Konstant, David M. Meyers, and Roderick B. Mast. *Lemurs of Madagascar*. Washington, D.C.: Conservation International, 1994.

Parsons, Michael. *The Butterflies of Papua New Guinea: Their Systematics and Biology*. San Diego: Academic, 1999.

Peterson, Dale. *The Deluge and the Ark: A Journey into Primate Worlds*. Boston: Houghton Mifflin, 1989.

Quammen, David. *The Song of the Dodo: Island Biogeography in an Age of Extinctions*. New York: Scribner's, 1995.

Schaller, George. *The Year of the Gorilla*. Chicago: University of Chicago Press, 1964.

Strahan, Ronald, ed. *The Mammals of Australia*. Sydney: Reed New Holland, 1998.

Wilson, E. O. *The Diversity of Life*. Cambridge, Mass.: Harvard University Press, 1992.

Yule, H., ed. and trans. *The Travels of Marco Polo: The Complete Yule-Cordier Edition*. Vol. 1. New York: Dover, 1993.

INDEX OF ANIMALS

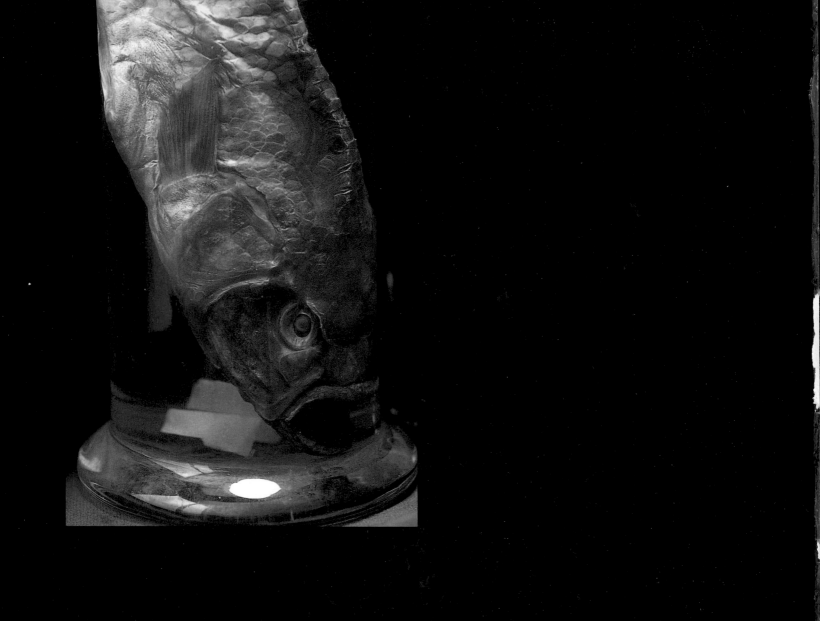